IMAGES
of England

# WEST YORKSHIRE
## COALFIELD

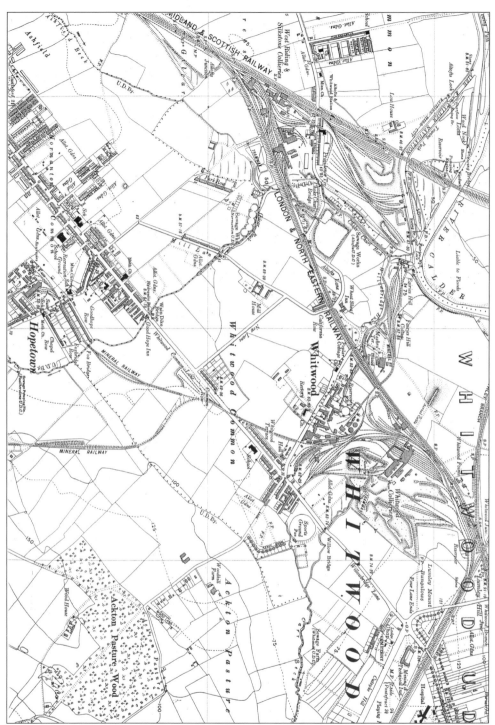

Whitwood, a large West Yorkshire colliery, *c*.1930, showing its relationship to the local railway and waterway system, its housing, its internal railway system and the associated gasworks and, at Hopetown, chemical works. In 1926 the colliery gave employment to some 2,859 men and boys below ground and 807 on the surface.

IMAGES
*of England*

# WEST YORKSHIRE
# COALFIELD

*Compiled by*
John Goodchild M. *Univ.*

TEMPUS

First published 2000
Copyright © John Goodchild, 2000

Tempus Publishing Limited
The Mill, Brimscombe Port,
Stroud, Gloucestershire, GL5 2QG

ISBN 0 7524 1745 2

Typesetting and origination by
Tempus Publishing Limited
Printed in Great Britain by
Midway Clark Printing, Wiltshire

# Acknowledgements

The author wishes to thank all those who, over the last fifty years, have given to him books, manuscripts, maps and illustrations relating to West Yorkshire (and others) collieries, some of which are used in this book. Others have been found in derelict buildingsor purchased from dealers or others.

# Contents

# Introduction

The story of the development of the West Yorkshire coalfield, like the story of any onetime inland and landlocked English coalfield, falls essentially into three parts. The first period extends from Roman times to the opening of inland navigation, with its facility for carrying coals cheaply to markets outside the coalfield area. The second sees the development of inland waterways, which begins in West Yorkshire with the opening of the Aire & Calder Navigation, under its Act of 1699, from the tideway to Leeds and to Wakefield in 1700 and around 1702 respectively, followed by the opening of a network of inland waterways which connected not only West Yorkshire with the North Sea beyond Hull, but also with three trans-Pennine canals, opened between 1804 and 1816. The new waterway system opened up the increasingly coal-hungry West Yorkshire industrial area, where there was greatly increased demand for coal from new or much enlarged old industries and from the growing local population. The third period was that of the railways, and later too of the motor lorry, when even larger coal markets developed and West Yorkshire began to serve not only London (which had been served only minimally earlier) and the south of England, but also industrial Lancashire and Europe and beyond.

The greatly improved transport facilities provided by the waterways and then the railways were quickly appreciated and exploited by coal capitalists, resulting in a huge expansion of coal output and increase in the number of West Yorkshire collieries. There were also areas of the county itself which, enjoying agricultural improvement from the eighteenth century, demanded increasing quantities of coal but were too far from inland waterways to use the large new collieries, which lay of necessity close to the waterways. Collieries, some with considerable output capacity, were opened specifically to serve these more isolated markets and, from the second half of the eighteenth century onwards, experiments were being made in working coal beyond the edge of the magnesian limestone ridge which effectively forms the modern border of the modern administrative county of West Yorkshire and formed the eastern boundary of the area of the exposed coalfield. Further small, rural collieries were opened to serve primarily local needs.

Any large colliery at the end of the eighteenth century had to provide housing for its new, largely immigrant workforce and their families. Initial scattered housing was sometimes followed by the building of new villages of colliers' cottages, with the necessary social ancillaries of school, shop and chapel. The workforce came largely from outside areas: some of those who arrived in the industrially disturbed 1860s and stayed were imported as blacklegs.

The very variety in the size and circumstances of collieries in West Yorkshire gave rise to a range of situations by the nineteenth century: one colliery might be predominantly supplying a local mill (or even be owned by one), another might primarily supply the coal needs of a large town, and yet another might supply – in part – almost worldwide markets. One colliery might be a drift, employing less than a handful of men and boys, another comprise a series of shafts working under one ownership, and a third be a big, deep colliery with only two shafts. The variety within the one coalfield was enormous.

The modern county of West Yorkshire, formed in 1974, lies within only a part of the ancient West Riding, which included not only the West and South Yorkshire coalfields, but outlying fields, from Sedburgh, Ingleton, Littondale and Kirkby Malzeard in the north, and the Forest of Bowland and Saddleworth in the west. The West Yorkshire coalfield which is our concern here has historical reality from at least the second half of the nineteenth century: the coalmasters' association and the men's union (until 1881, when the West and South Yorkshire men's associations joined) used this area of the West Yorkshire coalfield in their concerns, and since 1974 the boundary of the county has encompassed virtually all the West Yorkshire coalfield within its constituent Metropolitan Districts of Bradford, Calderdale, Kirklees, Leeds and Wakefield. The modern boundary is very similar to the geological extent of the exposed West Yorkshire coalfield, which extends from the valley of the Aire in the north to a little to the north of Barnsley, where it joins that of South Yorkshire; in the mid-nineteenth century this was the effective northern limit of the working of the Barnsley bed of coal, although in practice the Barnsley seam was worked within West Yorkshire too from the 1870s onwards.

The process of coal mining has always been an epic story of man contending with a variety of forces, geological, physical and social, and the purpose of this book is to illustrate some of these aspects of the industry. The history of the coalfield itself is very diverse: the thickness, qualities, depth and wetness of the seams worked, the working methods used, financial success or failure, transport facilities and all manner of other details differed between collieries. Hence this book can only hint at the significance of some of these factors: others have been considered by the author in a number of other publications.

Industrial pictorial evidence, the basis of this book, is comparatively rare in West Yorkshire, and there are few illustrations of local collieries before the end of the nineteenth century. Even later collieries were not generally recognised as being picturesque subjects by either photographers or painters. However, this book does attempt to illustrate something of the long history of the coalfield, using pictures and some illustrative documents and plans, with of course an explanatory text. The illustrations are entirely from the author's collection, at his unique Local History Study Centre at Wakefield, where they form part of a huge collection relating to the area. Further documents and information on the coalfield itself and on a great number of its individual collieries – as well as those of South Yorkshire – are available to users of the collection, by appointment and free of charge.

The generally smaller collieries in the northern and western part of the coalfield were even less likely to have been recorded in pictures than those further south, so this book, while recording collieries which were among the largest producers in the coalfield, cannot give a complete pictorial coverage and include pictures, say, of the numerous drift mines in the valleys above Huddersfield.

The story of coal mining within the West Yorkshire coalfield must include a consideration not only of the mining of coal, but also of the getting of associated products such as clay, ganister, fireclay, alum, iron ore and even sand for glassmaking – substances worked with, or in close physical association with, coal. Market forces have always been of major significance: coal has always been worked with a view to making a profit and, as collieries large or small have become exhausted or uneconomic, and as the markets for their coal have changed, contracted or disappeared, so they have closed. Rivalry between coalmasters has had major effects in the past, and today the skeletal regional coal industry has to contend with the loss of the domestic heating market. The collapse of the coal-based ancillary industries – of textiles manufacturing and processing, of engineering and ironfounding and iron and steel making, of glassworks, coke ovens, potteries, brickworks, and limeworks, among others, has been a major factors in the industry's decline in the twentieth century. Many of these industries have gone completely, others have diminished, still others have changed to other types of heat provision. The opencast coal industry does survive, despite spirited opposition to it on conservation grounds: it is of ancient origin, but always short term in its operation, if not in its effects.

The antiquity of coal working in West Yorkshire goes back at least as far as Roman times. It is known that the Romans worked coal at Garforth, at the north east corner of the large exposed coalfield, which they used in York at their crematoria. Workings with Roman remains are said to have been found at Thorpe on the Hill, near Rothwell, and coal was used by the Romans in their settlement at Castleford (Lagentium). Even in remote antiquity it was recognised that the coal which lay exposed at the surface outcrop of the seams, exposed to centuries of rain and frost, was of inferior quality to that which lay below ground and could only be reached by digging into the seam.

When local documentation first becomes available, in the thirteenth century, the number of references to coal in documents suggests that that the industry was widespread in West Yorkshire, that it was extensive, but not intensive in its nature. As much of West Yorkshire was well-forested, coal seems to have been used where timber provided an insufficient intensity of heat – especially for the working of iron (blacksmithing rather than iron smelting) and for the firing of pottery and other clay-based wares. Domestic use on a widening scale came later, along with increased use for various textile processes and other industrial purposes like limeburning, cokemaking for malting and brickmaking. Collections of records such as those of the huge Manor of Wakefield (well-recorded from 1274), the Duchy of Lancaster of the Elizabethan period, coroners inquest returns from the 1360s, or those connected with the fining of Royalists after the Civil Wars towards the end of the 1640s, or even the registrations of Papists' estates after the failure of the 1715 rebellion, essentially random as they all are, show the extensive nature of coal mining in the West Riding, as do the papers of individual estate and landowners. Whether coal was mined between the Roman period, ending in about 410 AD, and the first surviving documentary references from the early thirteenth century is not known, although archaeology has the potential to uncover evidence of such usage.

In the West Yorkshire coalfield, comparatively few owners of extensive estates (with coal beneath them), ventured their own capital in coal mining, preferring to allow the outlay and risk to rest on the shoulders of capitalists. Even where large scale coal mining was undertaken by a landowner, it was often for a short period – as with the Lowthers of Swillington Hall, or the Watertons of Walton Hall, although the Earls of Westmorland at Sharlston (and for a time on Wakefield Outwood) and their predecessors worked their own coal from the seventeenth century into the nineteenth. From the early nineteenth century the Lister Kayes of Denby Grange (between Wakefield and Huddersfield) worked their own coal on a large scale, into the modern period of steam-powered railways; so too did the Winns of Nostell Priory (ennobled in 1885 as Barons St Oswald), sinking new pits in the 1860s close to their older ones. In the eighteenth century Roger Crowle of Fryston Hallsank pits, unsuccessfully, below the magnesian limestone. The Gascoignes of Parlington Hall also worked their own coal, close to the Leeds & Selby Railway, the first modern railway in the West Riding, opened in 1834. But major landed families like the Tempests of Tong, the Barons Stourton (owners of the Rothwell Haigh estate), the Dukes of Leeds, the Earls of Cardigan and Dartmouth, the Wentworths of Woolley, the Beaumonts of Bretton and those of Whitley Beaumont – and others – preferred to allow others to make the investment in opening out their coals. The Brandlings of Middleton near Leeds worked their own coal from the seventeenth century until the mid-nineteenth century, when they failed and sold out; they were also associated with major Tyneside colliery interests.

The papers relating to the fining of ex-Royalists of the mid-seventeenth century and those appertaining to the estates of Roman Catholics from 1717 show that even the most rurally-situated and socially conservative landowners recognised the value of the coal underlying their estates and worked it themselves or via tenant coalmasters. There were also areas of small freeholder coal mining in West Yorkshire, where small scale mining occurred. These were to cause complications in the nineteenth century owing to the large numbers of leases from small freeholders involved in larger scale coal mining enterprises, and the attendant legal costs. It was recognised, however, that coal mining, especially after the opening of larger markets with the coming of artificial waterways from 1700, could offer very substantial rewards. The growing wealth of the Fenton family, almost entirely workers of coal under others' land, with a coal empire stretching from the Leeds area down through Wakefield to near Rotherham, and into Derbyshire, Nottinghamshire, and Leicestershire (with outlying concerns in South Wales and associated copper mining activity in Cornwall), was a demonstration of the wealth to be made from the combination of money, judgement and growing markets: William Fenton, the Coal King, was said to be worth well over £1 million at his death in 1837. Even earlier a modest landsale colliery near Flockton had produced sufficient for Richard Carter to build and endow a chapel, school and almshouses in the village by 1700.

Many of the newly rich colliery owners owned little land themselves, preferring to lease coal (effectively, of course, a purchase), and many, like the Fentons, never even lived in houses of which they held the freehold. Some dynasties of coalmasters managed to survive the 'rags to rags in three generations' syndrome: the Fentons only failed to find successful family successors after some 130 years, and the Charlesworths remained at the head of their sometime huge business from the 1770s until nationalisation of the coal industry in 1947, becoming, like the Fentons, gentlemen in standing and interests, although retaining active coal mining interests and abilities. The Briggs family was in a similar position, with coal mining interests in the family again extending from the 1770s to beyond 1947, the family producing some outstandingly able men and women.

Those landowners who preferred to let the working of their coal derived, in the case of successful colliery tenants, substantial income as coal rents, from which they were able to maintain their own standing. When a new area of coal was exploited, a landowner might suddenly become rich: a good example of this is the case of H.S.L. Wilson, the owner of Crofton Hall estate, who, once coal rents began to come in during the 1880s, was able to build huge, ugly extensions to his previously modest Georgian villa. The coal rents paid to the Barons Stourton, for example, must have considerably assisted their rebuilding of Allerton Park in Victorian medieval style – the house still stands – and have come in handy too, along with marriage settlement incomes, for maintenance, estate extension and provision of settlements for descendants.

Many of the coal seams of West Yorkshire derived their names from the locations which they outcropped the surface and where they were first worked on a considerable scale – thus the Haigh Moor (in West Ardsley), the Stanley Main, the Beeston, the Middleton, the Beamshaw (at Woolley Edge), the Flockton, and many another. Sometimes the seams were, for example, the Flockton Thick and Thin, or the Halifax Hard and Soft, according to their thickness or nature, or even the Low Moor (Bradford area) Better Bed and Black Bed, and so on.

Occasionally a seam name came from an early worker of the coal – as with the Wheatley Lime coal. It is less easy to identify the origins of other seam names – the Winter and Summer, the Cat and the Doggy, the Crow Coal – and a few bore names scarcely complimentary about the nature of the coal – the Lousy, the Muck, the Scale, the Stone Coal. Some coals were even assigned, for marketing purposes, names of coals well known but far distant from them – like the Silkstone or even the (Northumberland) Wallsend. The Diamond seam was a clever name to give a coal – it had nominal connections with 'black diamonds'.

Coal is a finite product and a colliery owner had to continuously identify and acquire new areas of coal to work. These were sometimes at a considerable distance, involving the opening of an entirely new and separate colliery. From the nineteenth century onwards the new location usually had better transport facilities than the old, but it often involved the provision of new housing and social infrastructure. Some colliery owners were also ironmasters or producers of bricks or clay products, ganister, fireclay, alum and iron, using the variety of raw materials their coalfields provided.

For the colliery capitalist and his financial backers, as for the new joint stock companies which brought in the capital necessary for the big new collieries of the railway period from the 1850s onwards, there were (as now) disturbing periods of both over-production and economic depression, and other periods of boom. Just as occasionally a colliery would make a net profit of fifty percent per annum in a boom time, in periods of depression prices for coal tumbled and difficulties were exacerbated by the consequent lowering of wages and the industrial unrest which naturally followed. Henry Briggs, Son & Co's 1865 experiment with profit-sharing with their workforce, which attracted international interest, resulted in part from their labour difficulties during periods of depression. The scheme later collapsed amid similar labour problems.

The shaft or drift mine was to find increasing competition in the last years of the private coal industry, from coal worked by opencast methods. Opencasting had occurred in the nineteenth century, albeit on a small scale and there was a temporary renewal of it during the General Strike period in 1926 and then a major development from 1942, as a result of war demand for coal. At nationalisation in 1947, those employing fewer than twenty-one underground workers remained as private, licensed mines. Their interesting story is documented in the writer's manuscript collections. The Second World War also witnessed the arrival of the Bevin Boy, and his story too is a fascinating one.

Perhaps reference should also be made to the role of women in coal mining locally. Although a few working girls and women remained to do pit top work – for example coal sorting at Sharlston colliery – most quickly disappeared from the time of the implementation of the Act of 1842 which prohibited them from working underground; some of them complained about the family financial difficulties which ensued. There were also women who were the widows or daughters of colliery owners who found themselves having to take up the reins of management – some of these are known of, and the little evidence shows that they were capable administrators. Even less frequent was the situation of the Denby Grange Colliery, where Lady Matilda Lister Kaye, an able and industrious woman, took an active part in the colliery's development during the lifetime of her more sportingly-minded husband and was followed by a daughter, the able Miss Emma.

The extent of the West Yorkshire coal industry has geographically changed in the twentieth century. Even before the forced closures of the 1980s the industry had almost disappeared from the upland western borders of the coalfield; the numerous small collieries (some also working clays) had become uneconomic – at the end of the Second World War there were many still at work in the Halifax area. Collieries in the vicinity of Penistone, the Spen Valley, and Huddersfield worked on into the period of nationalisation – when some of these had quite a large number of employees.

The West Yorkshire coal industry is now almost dead and it appears that, as a result of economic and planning difficulties, it will not revive in the foreseeable future. It is, however, an industry which has made a major contribution to the economic and physical development of the area, and its relics lie today on the ground and in documents, maps, illustrations and personal memories.

# *One*
# The Pre-Waterway Age

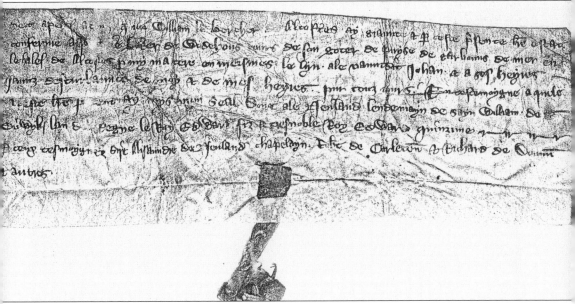

When locally produced documentation first becomes available to the historian, from the thirteenth century onwards, there are numerous references to an industry which was not only well-established, but fairly capital intensive. This deed of 1322, in Norman French, gives permission for the use of an underground water drainage tunnel, which suggests a colliery intended to be of some length of life, with money invested in its drainage.

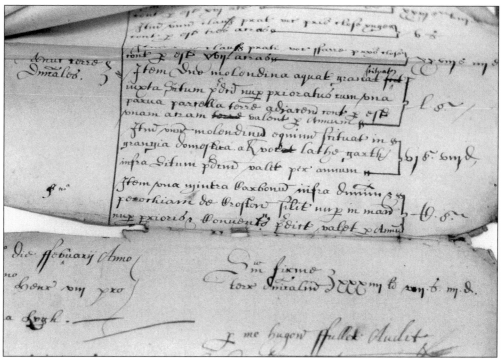

Late 1530s rent roll of Nostell Priory, showing a coal pit worked in the manor and parish of Crofton, lately in the hands of the Prior and Convent and worth £5 a year.

Some medieval coal workings were on a substantial scale, much more than mere holes working near-surface coal: they involved planning and capital expenditure. One of the pit tops of the extensive workings on Sharlston Common is shown here. The antiquity of coal mining is illustrated by an open strip field here being known as the Coal Pit Field, and by records of a coroner's inquest held in the fourteenth century into a death by a fall into a coal pit in Sharlston. The adjoining medieval timber-framed Sharlston Hall has a porch added by a coalmaster owner in 1574.

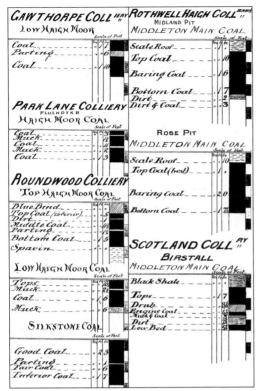
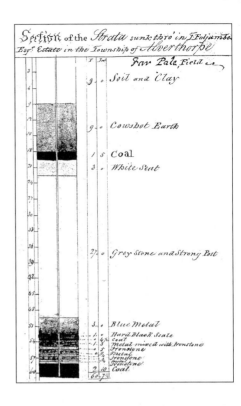

*Left:* Coal seams were only occasionally of one quality throughout, as this section of worked seams at five West Yorkshire collieries of around 1880 shows.

*Right:* Results of a coal-proving boring in around 1820.

Lease of a colliery at Crofton and land at Birkwood in 1596: the colliery was leased for twenty-one years at £21 a year plus forty wain loads of free coal paid yearly to the owner of Nostell Priory The rent of the land used was £1 a year. No more than two working pits and twelve workmen were to be employed, the workings and their drainage sough were to be maintained, and disused pits filled in.

*Left:* Collieries working before the later nineteenth century largely sorted their coal close to the working face underground, and their surface workings presented only small pit heaps, mostly the refuse from shaft sinking. The cost of underground carriage, coupled with the comparative shallowness of the workings, led to large numbers of shafts being (essentially successively) worked. This view of around 1880 shows the remains of spoil heaps of pits worked by the Fentons, the Coal Kings of the West Riding, from the 1770s, close to Lindle Hill, near Wakefield.

*Above and right:* Modern opencast coal workings often reveal substantial traces of earlier coal mining. Here at Kirkhamgate near Wakefield are remains of bellpit workings of unknown date; the lower picture shows the workings which may date from reworking in the same area of around the end of the eighteenth century. The photographs were taken in the 1990s.

# Two
# West Yorkshire Collieries

Bruntcliffe Victoria Colliery near Morley – yet another West Yorkshire colliery with the name of Victoria – was leased in 1846 and two shafts sunk between 1848 and 1850. It came to have its own branch to the GNR's main line and to possess three successive locomotives. In 1923 it employed 430 men and boys, but closed in 1929.

142.11. Featherston Main Colliery.

Featherstone Main Colliery was worked under part of the estate of George Bradley, who opened the nearby Featherstone Manor or Ackton Hall Colliery himself. The lease to John Shaw, a young coalmaster from Sheffield, was signed in 1874; the Shaws later came to own the South Kirkby, Featherstone Main, Ackton Hall and Hemsworth Collieries. Featherstone Main closed in 1930.

ROTHWELL HAIGH COLLIERY, Shewing OLD CASTLE, 1447.

The Rose and Fanny pits of J.&J. Charlesworth on Rothwell Haigh were said to have been named after Charlesworth daughters, although the evidence is uncertain. Again, although in rural surroundings, coal had been worked in the immediate area much earlier. The Rose pit was sunk in around 1850 (between 1847 and 1853), and the Fanny in around 1867, with the Beeston pit following in 1870. The Rothwell Haigh Colliery, of which these pits were the later manifestation, finally closed in 1983. The picture includes the few remains of the so-called Rothwell Castle, in fact a hunting lodge of the medieval hunting park of Rothwell Haigh.

East Ardsley Colliery lay adjacent to the ironworks there, but was differently owned; both adjoined the Bradford, Wakefield & Leeds Railway, opened in 1857, but which became in 1866 part of the new and direct GNR main line between London and Leeds. There had been numerous collieries here in the eighteenth century: some were connected to the Navigation by what was probably the world's first public railway, owned by the first railway company, the Lake Lock Rail Road, opened in 1798 However, these collieries had closed before East Ardsley was sunk: the first shaft was opened in about 1875. It closed in 1968, when it had just over 300 employees.

Hemsworth Colliery had a chequered history. Close to the site of earlier shallow workings and adjoining the new West Riding & Grimsby Railway (opened in 1866), two London coal merchant partners sank a new colliery which opened in mid-1877 and by 1879 had nearly 300 employees. In 1879 the promoters failed, but the colliery was carried on by the liquidator until 1890 and was then sold and much developed. By 1903 it had 1,651 employees. The colliery finally closed after merging with South Kirkby colliery in 1967.

Snydale Colliery was opened by Rhodes & Dalby in 1862 and purchased in 1897 by Henry Briggs, Son & Co. Briggs also bought, for a substantial £55,000, the adjoining Whitwell Main Colliery which had been sunk at a record pace in some six and a half months in 1868 to 228.5 yards. Whitwell Main was closed in the 1880s, although the local pub still bears the name of the Whitwell Main; Snydale Colliery was closed in 1965, employing then 380 men.

Surface and pit bottom at the new Frickley Colliery. Sunk in a hitherto sparsely inhabited area in 1903-1905, it worked a virgin area of coal and had excellent railway connections. The view of the pit bottom is an unusual subject for a picture postcard.

*Next page:* Coal had been worked in ancient times at Garforth – coal from that area has been identified as used to fire Roman crematoria at York. The opening of the Leeds & Selby Railway (the West Riding's first modern railway) in 1834 offered opportunities beyond the earlier agricultural markets to the north. The Sisters pit of the colliery was opened in 1843 and worked out in 1922; the Isabella pit was sunk in 1831-1833 and closed in 1925. The pits were named after the heiress owners of the estate and its collieries.

18

ISABELLA PIT GARFORTH.

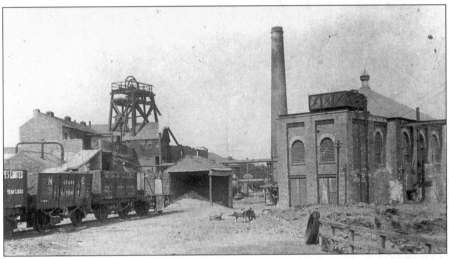

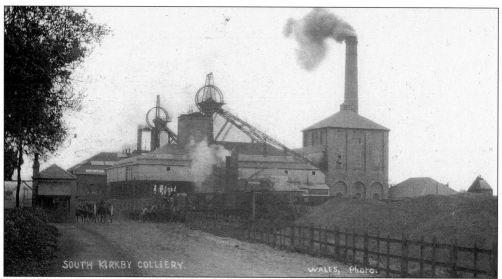

South Kirkby colliery was opened in an area hitherto purely agricultural and described as 'terra incognita' as far as coal mining potential was concerned. The lease was granted in 1874, just before the onset of the great depression. Its promoters were a large firm of Cleveland ironmasters, but they and the colliery failed in 1879. The colliery was reopened in 1881 and worked until 1988.

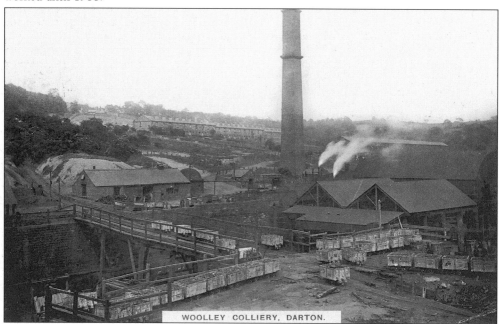

Coal had been worked under the great sandstone bluff of Woolley Edge on a sometimes large, albeit sporadic, scale since soon after the opening of the Aire and Calder Navigation to Wakefield in around 1702 and, on a small scale, even earlier. Yet it was the opening of the branch railway from Wakefield to Barnsley in 1850 which led the major local landowner to advertise his coalfield to let in 1852; it was leased, after negotiations with others, to the new Woolley Coal Company in 1853. They produced coal from drift workings, in 1854, working the Barnsley Bed – nearly 10ft in thickness here – and later other, less thick seams. Woolley colliery closed in 1987.

*Above and below:* Howley Park colliery lay adjacent to the main Leeds, Dewsbury & Manchester (later LNWR) railway line and was opened under a lease signed in 1849. It initially worked the Stone Coal (some 38in) and the Black or Flockton coal (27in) and other seams later. It had a succession of owners, including a number of mill owners anxious to secure coal supplies for textile manufacturing processes. It closed, exhausted, in 1928. The photographs show the screens, one of the wooden headgears, and horse-shunting in the colliery yard.

Glasshoughton Colliery and the associated coke and chemical works viewed from the air, c.1930. Prince of Wales Colliery, close to Pontefract, sunk in 1869-1872 and still at work today, is in the top background. Glasshoughton Colliery closed in 1986.

Glasshoughton Colliery, near Castleford, was sunk under a lease of 1865 and opened from 1869 to the Haigh Moor seam at 347 yards. It was the first modern colliery in the vicinity of Pontefract, although coal had been worked from the upper seams in that area since medieval times. It became a large and prosperous concern and was sold in 1902 for £115,000. This view of the colliery dates from about 1900.

A drawing of the colliery village of Loscoe near Normanton. The cottages here were built by a speculative builder and sold off to private investors, who then let them to Henry Briggs, Son & Co. who in turn let them to their colliers. The houses were built in 1873-1874.

A pencil drawing of the 1840s showing the view from Hartfeild Hall, near Wakefield. The plumes of smoke are from collieries, a gothic-style pumping engine house and limekilns; on the right, coal wagons pass along a colliery tram road opened in about 1837.

The first sods for Wrenthorpe Colliery's shafts were cut early in 1838. It was closed in 1900 after the death of W.T. Marriott, its owner, but was bought by the Low Laithes Colliery in 1905 and re-opened by them in 1907, being used as part of their principal colliery. It had a branch line to the nearby main Leeds-London railway; this section opened in 1857. Low Laithes Colliery closed in 1928. The picture is reproduced from a torn and tiny print.

A modern view of Woolley colliery, with its vast spoil heaps towering above both the colliery and the nearby M1 motorway.

South Kirkby colliery as photographed for the British Mining Industry supplement to the *Daily Telegraph* of 16 September 1930.

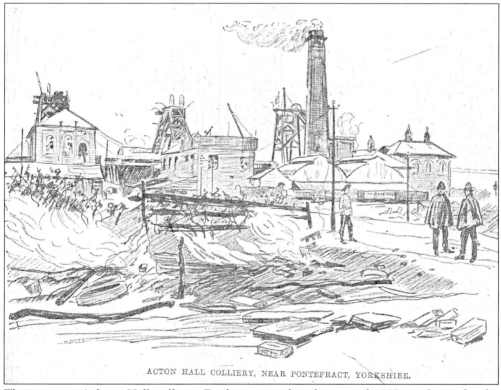

ACTON HALL COLLIERY, NEAR PONTEFRACT, YORKSHIRE.

The scene at Ackton Hall colliery, Featherstone, after the riot of 1893, as drawn for the *Illustrated London News*.

*Above and below:* Howroyd Colliery, close to Lower Whitley near Dewsbury, closed in 1962, when it employed forty men. It had been opened between 1903 and 1907, and Howroyd New Colliery was opened in the later 1920s. This was a typically-located Pennine foothill drift colliery; it survived nationalisation and is shown here in photographs taken in 1967.

No. 1728.—VOL. LXI.    SATURDAY, OCTOBER 19, 1872.    WITH EXTRA SUPPLEMENT (COLOURED) } SIXPEN BY POST,

THE MORLEY MAIN COLLIERY, NEAR DEWSBURY, AFTER THE EXPLOSION.

An explosion occurred at Morley Main Colliery in October 1872, killing thirty-four men and boys. The surface scene after the explosion was drawn by an artist *for The Illustrated London News* and appeared in its issue of 19 October 1872: it shows families and relatives awaiting the removal of bodies from the workings.

27

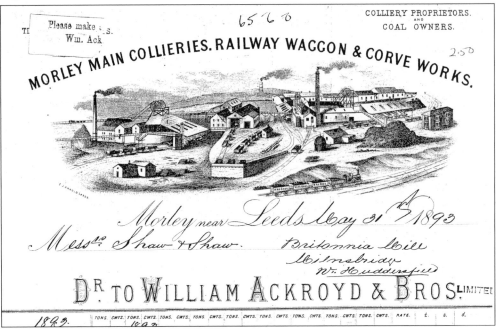

Morley Main Colliery lay close to the town of Morley and the main Leeds-Manchester (LNWR) railway, opened in 1848. Coal was worked in Morley in ancient times, but this large colliery – it employed some 1,000 men and boys in 1893 – was opened under a coal lease of 1854 and closed in 1909. It was the scene of a colliery disaster which killed thirty-four in 1872, and of riots during the miners' strike of 1893. Its position enabled it to serve, like many other West Yorkshire collieries, Lancashire coal markets. Morley Main had its own wagon and coal tub works.

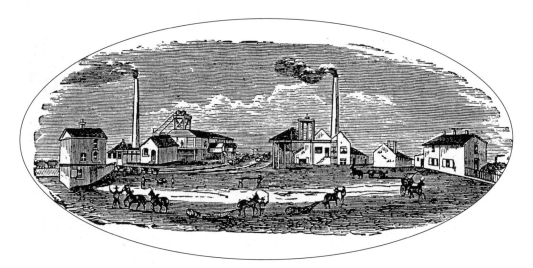

One of the Bowling Iron Company's many coal and ironstone pits to the south of Bradford. This is probably one of their Hunsworth pits: the view appeared in Johnnie Gray's book *One Hundred and Eighty Pleasant Walks around Bradford*, 1880. The company had an extensive railway system which connected its pits with the main works, and this view shows the railway and the wagons on it as well as the coal screens.

J.&J. Charlesworth worked collieries in both the West and South Yorkshire coalfields, and on a large scale; indeed they succeeded the Fentons as the Coal Kings of Yorkshire. This view is of their Robin Hood Colliery, adjoining the Leeds to Wakefield main road. The colliery was sunk in 1830-1831 and remained in Charlesworth hands until nationalisation in 1947. The photograph was taken in connection with an early motor car accident; here a branch of the East & West Yorkshire Union Railway (Charlesworth-promoted) crossed the road and the electric tramway rails. The pumping engine was a Cornish type, 65in cylinder, lifting from about 420ft and of 120hp.

Ackton Hall Colliery in 1893, on the occasion of a Section visit at a meeting of the British Association for the Advancement of Science in that year.

Wheldale Colliery, near Castleford, was sunk from 1868 and, despite financial and administrative difficulties, became a large colliery employing, with its sister colliery at Fryston, 3,156 men and boys in 1911. Fryston closed in 1985, Wheldale in 1987. The pictures show a general view of Wheldale, and detail of its steam winding engine.

Wheldale Colliery winding engine: a close-up view.

Caphouse pit (now the National Coal Mining Museum), alongside the Wakefield & Austerlands (via Huddersfield) ex-turnpike road. The scene today is little different.

In the colliery yard at Caphouse pit of the Denby Grange Colliery. The twin headstocks, the coal screens and the gangway for spoil to the heap are clearly shown.

Old Roundwood Colliery near Wakefield, again in an area where coal had been mined for centuries from the upper seams, was sunk in 1853 – the sinking agreement for the 9ft and 10ft shafts survives. The colliery was connected by its own branch railway to the outside world from 1862, and continued to work until 1966. Originally named Roundwood, it adopted the additional Old when a new South Yorkshire colliery, also called Roundwood, got into financial difficulties.

The modern steel headgear at Sharlston Colliery. On a medieval coal mining site, modern shafts were sunk under a lease of 1858 and subsequently deepened so considerably that a two-lift system had to be used for winding purposes. A colliery village was built – and it still survives, with its chapel, school and co-op buildings. The colliery closed after the great strike of the 1980s.

Manor Colliery near Wakefield achieved a record output of four tons per man per shift in 1973, when it employed 221 men. It closed in 1981.

Something to cheer about at Manor Colliery.                    (W1762/1)

# Mini-pit soars above national output rate

Newmarket Colliery was sunk in 1836-1837 for J.&J. Charlesworth and was owned and worked by them until nationalisation in 1947. It closed in 1983 and was then one of the country's oldest working collieries.

*Left and below:* The railway and electric tramway crossing outside Robin Hood Colliery, near Rothwell, witnessed an early motor car accident: these photographs were taken in connection with the subsequent legal proceedings.

*Above and below:* A temporary opencast coal working at Emley Moor near Huddersfield, opened during the great strike of 1926. At the head of the inclined plane coal was offloaded onto road lorries. A number of such temporary workings were opened by opportunists to provide coal not otherwise available because of the strike.

Bramwyn No.1 Colliery – or Peggy Tub Main – was a small landsale colliery opened at Durkar, near Wakefield, in 1945 or early in 1946, and closed in 1951. It was to become one of the first Small Mines, exempted from nationalisation from the beginning of 1947. The make-do-and-mend nature of its structures will be noted.

Parkhill Colliery near Wakefield in 1983, the year of its closure. Opened in 1877, again in an area where there had been earlier coal mining, it was served by both railway and navigation, and had its own coal yard close to the industrialised town of Wakefield. It had been a very 'wet' colliery, and in its early days part of its pumping costs had been met by the nearby Normanton Local Board, who in return received a public supply of its water.

*Above and below:* In typical earlier nineteenth-century fashion, the Victoria Colliery consisted of a number of working pits strung out along a railway of some two miles between the village of Outwood and the Navigation basin at Stanley Ferry. The collieries finally closed in about 1896; these photographs show the furthermost of the pits, at Newton Lane End Outwood, *c*.1890. The name of Victoria as applied to a colliery was a common occurrence; this colliery was opened in 1837 and was probably the largest of West Yorkshire's numerous Victorias.

Newmillerdam Colliery, a photograph taken in 1983, after its closure in 1981. Coal had been worked in the area since at least the seventeenth century, sporadically, and the modern colliery originated with the Nineveh Colliery here of the 1920s.

The earliest Yorkshire colliery photograph known to the author is this showing Briggs' Methley Junction Colliery, near Leeds. It may date from the 1860s.

Briggs' Whitwood Colliery's Speedwell Yard, perhaps about 1870. Note the old shaft in the background: is demolition work taking place there? The amount of timber in the foreground suggests that major colliery construction work is underway.

Briggs' Whitwood Colliery's Speedwell Yard with its central workshops, c.1900.

**HOLLINGTHORPE,**

CRIGGLESTONE, nr. WAKEFIELD.

**TO COAL MASTERS AND OTHERS.**

# CATALOGUE

OF THE VALUABLE

## COLLIERY PLANT;

### STEAM ENGINES;

### BOILERS;

#### WEIGHING MACHINES;

#### IRON RAILING;

#### MEMEL & OTHER TIMBER;

#### BLACKSMITHS' TOOLS, ETC., ETC.,

WHICH WILL BE

## SOLD BY AUCTION,

## BY MR. T. CRAWSHAW,

On Tuesday, March 27th, 1860,

At the Hollingthorpe Colliery.

Sale to commence at 11 o'clock in the Forenoon.

*Wool-market, Pontefract, March 19th, 1860.*

John D. Littlefield, Printer, Pontefract.

Catalogue of the equipment of a colliery at Hollingthorpe, Crigglestone, in 1860.

IN THE MATTER OF THE WOOLLEY MOOR COLLIERY COMPANY, LIMITED, IN LIQUIDATION.

SALE BY TENDER AS A GOING CONCERN.

THE WHOLE of the COLLIERY PREMISES and COLLIERY PLANT and TOOLS of the above Company are offered for sale by Tender as a going concern.

The Colliery is situate about 4 miles from Wakefield and 7 from Barnsley and Dewsbury, and comprises the Lessees Interest in the unexpired Leases of the Mapplewell or Kent Thick Seam, comprising 204 acres and in the unexpired Lease of the Upper Beamshaw Coal and Lower Beamshaw Coal (now exhausted) and of the surface rights in 1 acre, 1 rood, and 6 perches of Land at Carters Spa, Crigglestone, and in two pieces of Land containing together 4 acres, 1 rood, and 1 perch also situate at Carters Spa.

The Plant comprises Hauling Engines, Drums, Shafting and Gearing for main and tail haulage, Oil Engine, Cornish Boiler, W.I. Cisterns, 12 ton Weigh Bridge and 1 ton Corve Weigh, Horses, Harness and Carts, Saw Mill, Blacksmith's Tools, Corves, Pitrails, Turns and Flags, Piping, Wire Ropes, Miner's tools, stores, &c., and Brick and Wood erections forming Pit Bank and Screens, Offices, Engine Houses, Blacksmith's shop, Stables and Hay Chamber.

The Colliery is in actual work and will be handed over as a going concern.

Being worked from a Day-hole it can be run on unusually favourable terms, the cost of haulage, &c., being very small, and it offers an exceptional opportunity for Investment.

Tenders must be sent in to the Receiver and Liquidator, Mr. Tom Broadhead, Chartered Accountant, Dewsbury, on or before the first day of May, 1905.

Detailed particulars, with permission to view, and Tender forms may be obtained from the Receiver and Liquidator at his Offices, Borough Chambers, Dewsbury, or from

SCHOLEFIELD, TAYLOR & MAGGS,

Solicitors.

Batley.

Advertisement for a dayhole colliery and its plant in 1905.

Emroyd Common, Middlestown, where coal and ironstone were leased in the later 1790s and collieries and a blast furnace opened in 1803. The colliery at the top of the common closed in 1893, as did the steam-powered portion of its colliery railway, running along the centre of this picture.

Ruins of the Emroyd Common, Middlestown coke blast furnace, as surviving in the 1960s but later destroyed by opencast workings for coal.

Henry Briggs, Son & Co.'s new Saville Colliery at Methley was sunk during the coal boom of the early 1870s – a boom which was to be followed from 1874 by a prolonged period of depression in the industry. It was served by both railway and water transport and closed only in 1986.

Briggs' Don Pedro Colliery, abandoned in 1912 although only sunk some thirty years earlier; it subsequently remained in use as a fan pit.

Briggs' Methley Junction Colliery as it appeared at about the time of the First World War.

A lantern slide view of colliers at, apparently, a drift entrance – with their lamps.

Morley Main
Colliery yard, with
its stocks of pit
timber. The colliery
closed in 1909.

Pit top lads riding –
illegally – on empty
tubs as they run down
from the screens.

Building the headgear and the turbo alternator house at Altofts West Riding Colliery Silkstone pit, completed in 1900; one of a series of photographs showing the surface work in progress.

Drawings of Briggs' pit top tipplers and coal screens at Whitwood Colliery in 1913.

A group of officials with a plan of the new Silkstone pit workings, at Altofts West Riding Colliery, soon after 1900.

Altofts West Riding Colliery in 1977. The double gates had carried the railway branch to the staiths on the side of the Aire & Calder Navigation: the controlling signal can be seen.

*Above and below*: Underground colliery views are, by nature of their location, somewhat rare. Here are underground scenes in the collieries of the South Kirkby, Featherstone & Hemsworth Collieres Ltd, *c*.1912.

*Present and following page:* Further underground scenes in the South Kirkby, Featherstone & Hemsworth Collieries, c.1912.

# Sad memories of pit

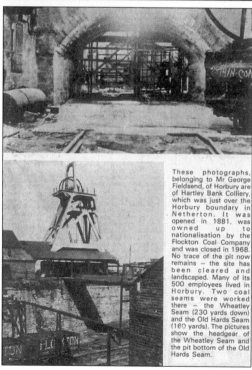

These photographs, belonging to Mr George Fieldsend, of Horbury are of Hartley Bank Colliery, which was just over the Horbury boundary in Netherton. It was opened in 1881, was owned up to nationalisation by the Flockton Coal Company and was closed in 1968. No trace of the pit now remains — the site has been cleared and landscaped. Many of its 500 employees lived in Horbury. Two coal seams were worked there — the Wheatley Seam (230 yards down) and the Old Hards Seam (160 yards). The pictures show the headgear of the Wheatley Seam and the pit bottom of the Old Hards Seam.

*Above and left*: Hartley Bank Colliery, with both railway and Navigation access, was opened near Horbury in 1873 and closed in 1968, then employing 478 men.

Shuttle Eye Colliery, at Grange Moor near Huddersfield, was at work by 1864. Its owner also kept the nearby Blacksmith's Arms Inn. It survived nationalisation and closed in 1973, then employing 220 men.

Denby Grange Colliery's Prince of Wales or, colloquially, the Wood pit, opened in around 1877. As it lay alongside an ascending inclined plane (for the loaded wagons), side guiders for the incline ropes were required for wagons entering or leaving the pit yard.

Briggs' Water Haigh Colliery at Oulton, near Leeds, sunk in 1910 and closed in 1970.

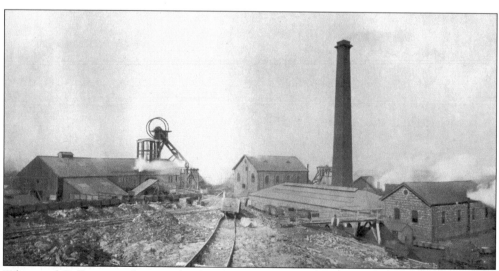

Whitwood Colliery – a photograph taken before 1900 – showing a tub on the spoil heap.

Shawcross Colliery, near Dewsbury, of Crawshaw & Warburton, sunk in 1903 and closed in 1968.

An engraved letterhead of the 1860s of Pope and Pearson, West Riding Colliery, Altofts.

The powerhouse at Whitwood Colliery, supplying electricity to the Whitwood area collieries of the concern.

# Three
# Transporting the Coal

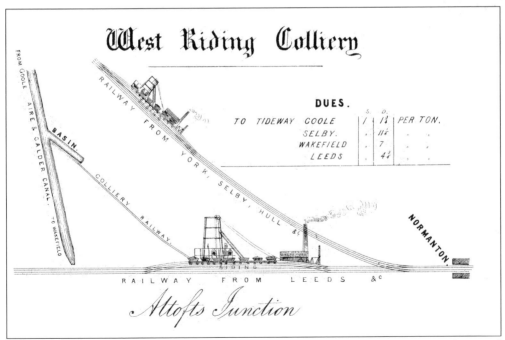

A letterhead showing the location of Altofts West Riding Colliery vis-à-vis its railway and waterway situation, and also showing the firm's slightly earlier colliery (first sod cut early in 1851) at Whitwood. The Popes were London coal merchants who removed first to work coal at Crigglestone and then on to the Normanton area, while George Pearson was an illiterate but financially successful railway building contractor. The washing of coal brought to the surface was carried out at this colliery from 1858 onwards, and coal cutting machines were investigated in 1860.

A boat leaving the entrance lock at Heath near Wakefield where the Barnsley Canal fell into the Aire & Calder Navigation, c.1900. The boat is empty, and was probably going up the canal to load with coal at Walton or one of the canal-side collieries. On the left is a horse marine and behind him the stabling and toll office of the canal; on the right are cock boats, used in tidal waters for access to the land, left behind here to be picked up by a returning boat.

The Stanley Ferry Basin of the Aire & Calder Navigation; a tramroad from Lofthouse Colliery brought coal for loading here until the mid-1920s. An old lady sits knitting, resting on the rudder of her boat, while other empty boats wait nearby.

'Pans' or compartment boats awaiting unloading at Goole: the postcard was used in 1906, but the compartment boat system was first used in 1865, and ultimately the Aire & Calder Navigation – who owned the Port of Goole – had just over 1,000 of them.

The twenty-arch stone viaduct on the Old Flockton Colliery's railway to Lane End Colliery. The viaduct was in existence by 1803 and was used until 1893; it survives.

St John's Colliery, near Normanton, had both standard staiths and a unique coal loading system onto the Navigation – as well as ordinary railway sidings. Here an empty compartment boat is being drawn on its bogie out of the Navigation at Stanley Ferry, on its way to be loaded at the colliery some 1.5 miles away. The system was introduced in 1891 and closed around 1941.

St John's Colliery: a compartment boat loaded with coal awaits lowering on its bogie into the Navigation.

The compartment boat system – essentially a railway train on the water – was introduced in 1865; initially each compartment carried 25 tons, but ultimately they carried 40 tons. Here compartments are being loaded at Allerton Bywater Colliery's staiths alongside the Leeds branch of the Aire & Calder Navigation.

A typical train of coal-laden compartment boats below Castleford. Up to nineteen compartments formed a single train.

The coal hoist, to lift waterway compartment boats and tip their contents into the holds of sea-going vessels, was an essential part of the compartment-boat system. The diagram shows the system in operation in the Port of Goole.

Top of the upper incline at Middleton near Leeds in 1956. The incline, built to carry coal from pits on the plateau above the earlier colliery's workings, was used latterly to carry coal uphill for sale in the new, largely council house, suburb of Middleton.

Leeds from the head of the lower incline of the Middleton Colliery railway, around 1840. The availability of coal was responsible for the possibility of the development of the glassworks,

pottery works, ironworks and textile works shown here in Hunslet.

The coal staiths serving the town of Leeds at the (later) lower end of the Middleton Colliery's wagonway, opened in 1758. The first railway Act of Parliament was passed in 1758 for some of the construction powers for this line. The photograph was taken in 1956 and the staith structure has recently been the subject of an archeological survey and excavation.

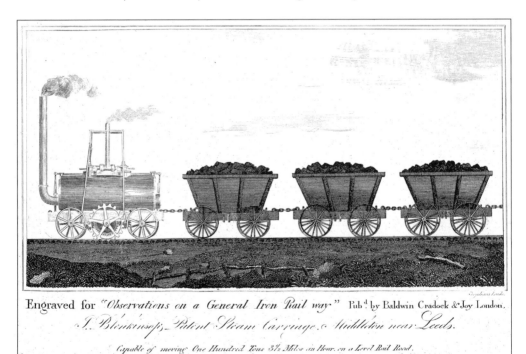

Engraved for "*Observations on a General Iron Rail way*" Pub.d by Baldwin Cradock & Joy London.

*J. Blenkinsop's Patent Steam Carriage. Middleton near Leeds.*

*Capable of moving One Hundred Tons 3½ Miles an Hour on a Level Rail Road.*

A more detailed engraving of one of the Middleton Colliery's railway locomotives and some of its wagons, in the 1820s. The locomotives drew themselves along by means of a rack rail, also shown here.

Lorry-carried coal being transferred to a boat in Thornes Lane, Wakefield, *c*.1956. The staith is said to have been built by German prisoners during the First World War.

Park Hill Colliery's sidings in 1912. Note the name of the company on the wagons and their use of the words 'Park Hill Wallsend Coal', a term used to suggest quality similar to that of the famous and well-patronised coals from Wallsend near Newcastle-upon-Tyne. The locomotive, named *Ninety*, was bought new in that year and had been built by Black, Hawthorn & Co. Ltd.

A railway coal wagon destination label from Briggs' Whitwood Colliery of 1853.

A locomotive builders' photograph of an engine supplied by Pecketts of Bristol. She is said to have been supplied in 1922 for Newlands St John's Colliery, near Normanton, but does not appear on their list of locomotives in *Industrial Locomotives of Yorkshire (East and West Ridings)*, 1954.

The Denby Grange Colliery railway of 1854: No.1 winding engine, drawing loaded wagons up from the background and lowering them down towards the Navigation and railway.

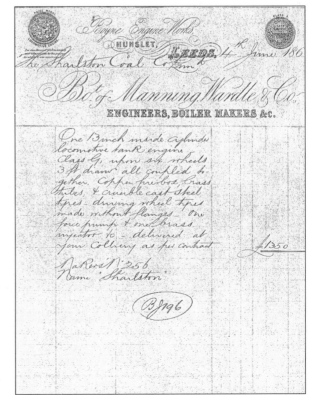

Locomotive power was expensive, but it was increasingly necessary for large collieries – even for those which lay close to mainline railways or waterways, or which supplied towns. Here the Sharlston Coal Company buys a new locomotive from a local firm with a wide market, in 1868.

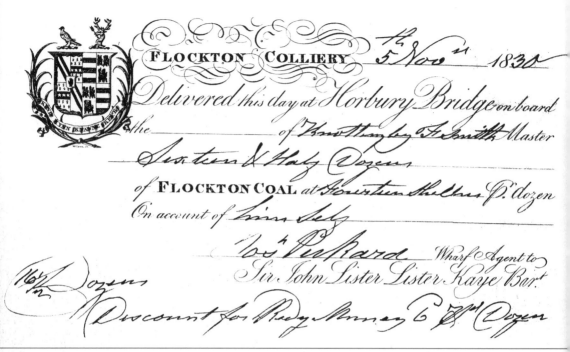

An unusually highly decorated delivery note for coal from Sir J.L.L. Kaye's Flockton (Denby Grange) Colliery in 1830.

Normanton railway sidings c.1900. The opening of three railway companies' routes, which by mere geographical chance met at Normanton, led to the village becoming a major interchange for both passengers and goods, while large, new, deep collieries were sunk alongside the new railways here in the 1840s, 1850s and 1860s. The sidings are now overgrown and without their rails, while the erstwhile important station is now a mere halt.

Coal ready for the industrialist: a view of the Calder Vale Road Yard adjoining Kirkgate
Station, Wakefield, with coal wagons loaded for the supply of the adjacent iron, glass and
chemical works, which had turntable access to them.

Ackton Hall or Featherstone Manor Colliery was opened in 1867 by George Bradley, the Castleford-based lawyer and entrepreneur, who had recently purchased the coal-rich Featherstone and Ackton estate. Coal had been worked hereabouts much earlier, and in the eighteenth century a steam pumping engine had been built to dewater the workings of a colliery which served the rich agricultural countryside to the south. It was Ackton Hall Colliery which witnessed the 1893 Featherstone Massacre, during coal mining based riots.

The well-known engraving published in 1829, showing the staiths of the railway opened in 1758 to bring coal from the Middleton Colliery to Leeds. The locomotive is one of the type introduced here in 1812 – they were the first practicable locomotives used in the world. The engine had a single chimney: the engraver has mistakenly assigned a background mill chimney to the engine.

An upset on the Denby Grange Colliery railway, perhaps in the 1880s. The railway, opened in 1854, was a strange one, combining normal steam traction with a tunnel, two sets of reversing necks and two sets of inclined planes, each up and down hill. It closed, except for a short lower section to the Navigation and railway, early in the 1940s.

The coal staiths on the Calder & Hebble Navigation of the Denby Grange Colliery's railway, opened in 1854, near Calder Grove, Wakefield.

The Wood pit of Denby Grange Colliery, lying alongside the railway opened in 1854. Note the fanhouse on the right.

The coal loading staiths at Methley Savile Colliery (Henry Briggs, Son & Co.), c.1903. The drop hoppers allowed coal to be loaded into boats in a way which prevented breakage of the large coal lumps.

# *Four*
# The Workers

A print of a Yorkshire collier with one of the Middleton colliery pits behind and one of its locomotives in the centre. The print was published in 1814, two years after the introduction of the regular use of locomotive power on the colliery's internal railway serving the town of Leeds.

A carving of a collier setting wooden chocks to support timbering above a pit prop. Behind the man are his lamp and water bottle.

Bower's Allerton Colliery, near Swillington in the lower Aire Valley, was the site of extensive colliery working in the upper seams in the eighteenth and early nineteenth centuries. It included the use of a number of steam pumping engines and early wagonways, but the equipment was sold off in 1843. The deeper coal was leased early in the 1850s to the Bowers, glassmasters in Hunslet, Leeds, but already also coalmasters, and the leases were renewed from 1873-1874, although the colliery was advertised for sale in 1879. The colliery closed in 1970 and it was by then known as Primrose Hill.

74

*Left and below*: Prosecution of the owners of Shibden Colliery in 1856, where several fatalities had occurred. They had not complied with the requirements of the Government Inspector of Mines in relation to establishing specific regulations for the colliery.

SATURDAY.—Before W. H. Rawson, Esq., and S. Waterhouse, Esq.

CONVICTIONS UNDER THE COAL MINES INSPECTION AMENDMENT ACT.

Messrs. Joseph and John Holt, occupiers of the Shibden Colliery, near Halifax, were summoned on informations laid against them by Charles Morton, Esq., Inspector of Coal Mines, and charged that on the 21st ult. they were guilty of of five distinct breaches of the act 18 and 19 Vict., chap. 108. Mr. Skipworth, of Wakefield, appeared on the part of the prosecution, and Mr. Mitchell represented the defendants.

Mr. Skipworth stated the nature of the charge, and explained the reasons which had led Mr. Morton to institute these proceedings. He was acting by the authority and direction of the Secretary of State for the Home Department, in carrying out an act of parliament of considerable importance in the mining districts. The act came into operation in August last, its provisions having been previously sifted and discussed before a select committee of the House of Commons. Its requirements must therefore be perfectly well-known to those interested in collieries. The first summons charged the defendants with the non-establishment of "special rules." The act declared that such "special rules" should be established in coal mines as might appear best calculated to prevent dangerous accidents. He need scarcely observe that before the passing of this act it must have been necessary and desirable to have rules for the guidance of miners,—rules by which each man might know what was his precise duty, and knowing it, be amenable to the law if he failed in the performance of it. In the present case he would show that Mr. Morton, in consequence of a fatal accident that occurred at the defendants' pit, called their attention in December, 1854, to the importance of establishing such rules. Mr. Skipworth then read a letter from the defendants, dated the 4th of January 1855, in which they promised to consult with the coal masters of the neighbourhood on the best code of rules to be established, and that as soon as these rules were drawn out, they should be printed and circulated among the workmen. Notwithstanding this promise made more than a year ago, there had been as yet no attempt to perform it. On the 21st of February last, another fatal accident occurred at the defendants' pit, to a boy named George Harewood, who was killed by falling down the shaft. The defendants informed the Secretary of State that it arose by the unfortunate youth having attempted to get out of the corf, contrary to their *rules*. The word "rules" was underlined, and implied that rules in accordance with the act of parliament had been established. This letter was sent by the Secretary of State to Mr. Morton, who applied to the defendants for a copy of the rules, and then the defendants admitted they had none. Mr. Skipworth would leave it to the magistrates to express an opinion upon the conduct of the defendants in this respect. The second information against the defendants was for not having published the "general rules" in accordance with the act, which provided that a copy of the special and general rules should be exhibited in some conspicuous part of the colliery office, and that a printed copy of the same should be supplied to every person employed in or about the colliery. The third information was for a breach of one of these "general rules," which declared that every working pit or shaft shall be provided with some proper means of signalling from the bottom of the shaft to the surface, and from the surface to the bottom of the shaft. Since the 21st of February, when the fatal accident happened, the defendants had provided themselves with an iron signal rod; but on that day there was no such thing. The 4th information charged the defendants with not complying with the provisions of the 6th "general rule,"

namely, that "a proper indicator to show the position of the load in the pit or shaft, and also an adequate break shall be attached to every machine worked by steam or water power, and for lowering or raising persons." When the Inspector went to the defendants' colliery, on the 7th of March, there was no indicator to be found, although a fatal accident had occurred there on the 21st of February. Instead of a proper indicator there was a piece of hemp on the pit rope, and the engine-man had to judge from the hempen mark how far the ascending corf was from the top of the pit. To shew how injurious this rude contrivance was in practice, he might say that a fatal accident, which occurred at a pit near Wakefield, only last month, was attributable, to a great extent, to this improper substitute for an indicator. He was reminded by the Inspector that pit ropes were frequently found to break at the point where the hempen mark was tied. Such an ineffectual mode of indication was objectionable on another ground. It might frequently happen (as occurred recently at a pit near Manchester) that the engine-man's eyes were not directed to the hempen mark at the precise moment, and he lost sight of it altogether, the result being that the corve was drawn to the pulley, from whence its unfortunate occupants were precipitated to the bottom of the shaft. The last charge was for a breach of the 7th "general rule," that "every steam boiler shall be provided with a proper steam gauge, water gauge, and safety valve." At the time of the informations being laid the defendants had no steam or water gauge, but they had since then provided them. This prosecution had arisen from the death which occurred on the 21st of Feb.; and the government Inspector had received instructions in every case where an accident occurred, to prosecute those who should be guilty of any breach of this law. Certain colliery owners were unwilling to incur the expense of complying with this act; legal measures were therefore the only means that could be adopted to compel them. He (Mr. S.) would leave it to the discretion of the bench to say what penalties they would inflict.

Mr. Mitchell, after complimenting Mr. Skipworth upon the mechanical skill and the professional talent he had brought to bear upon this case, said he had already consulted with him, and the result was that he, on behalf of his clients, pleaded guilty to the series of charges urged against them. This colliery had been under the sole direction of Mr. James Holt, who died a fortnight ago, and but for that gentleman's illness, during the last three or four months, they would not have been summoned there to-day. The Messrs. Holt were about complying with the requirements of the act of parliament when this unfortunate accident happened. Mr. Mitchell expressed a hope that the magistrates would act in a like manner to the magistrates at Wakefield, who in a similar case, imposed a fine of £5, on the first information, and nominal penalties of 6d. each on the others.

W. H. Rawson, Esq., said the defendants had shown their good judgment by pleading guilty to these offences. There could be no question that they had wilfully violated the law, and had not, in the slightest degree, attempted to comply with its provisions. The negligence was clearly wilful on their part. The magistrates fined them, on the first information, £5 and costs, and in each of the other cases £1 and costs, and he hoped it would go forth to the public that there was such an act of parliament, and that it was considered of the utmost importance by the bench that its provisions should be obeyed, not only by the Messrs. Holt, but by all colliery workers in this and every other district. The magistrates were determined to assist the Inspector in carrying out, in every possible way, the provisions of this humane act of parliament.

Charles Morton (1811-1882) was appointed one of the first four HM Inspectors of Mines in 1850, with responsibilities including Yorkshire. He was a Sheffield man and had been a colliery manager, then a partner with Henry Briggs in the new Whitwood Colliery, before setting up his own consultative business and being appointed an Inspector. He held that office until retiring from ill health occasioned by the Oaks Colliery disaster of 1866. Like Briggs, he was a Unitarian and a Liberal.

A group of colliery employees of the Denby Grange collieries near Huddersfield, the date is apparently soon after 1900.

A group of colliers at Low Laithes Colliery, Gawthorpe, near Ossett. The date of the photograph is unknown. The colliery was opened in 1892, using enlarged earlier shafts; it closed in 1928 and had a long connecting railway to nearby Flushdyke Station – a colliery railway on which, it is said, excursion trains from Gawthorpe were run.

Colliery pay identity discs, used at Woolley Colliery before, and at Park Hill after, nationalisation.

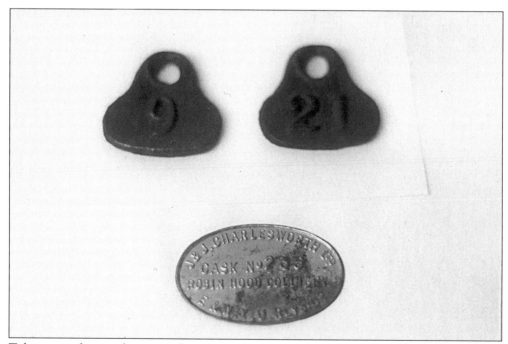

Tub motties from early-twentieth-century opencast workings near Ossett, and a barrel label from Robin Hood Colliery, with the initials of the East & West Yorkshire Union Railways which served that colliery and its coke and by-products plant.

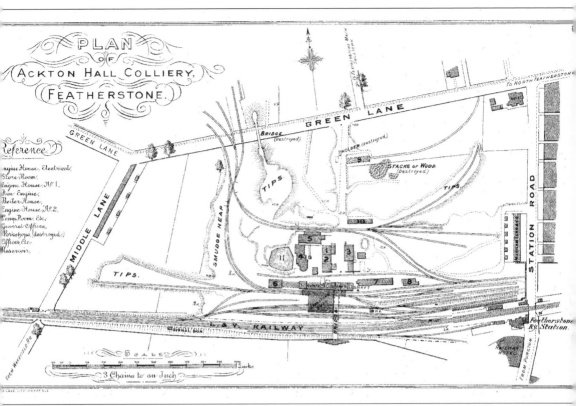

The location of the Featherstone Massacre of 1893, when two men were killed by fire from the military attending a riot there in that riot-stricken year in the West Yorkshire coalfield. A government inquiry, of a whitewashing nature, followed the deaths.

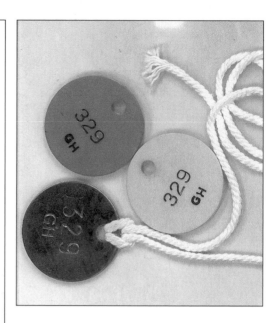

NATIONAL COAL BOARD - North Yorkshire Area

## EMERGENCY ORGANISATION

Serial N⁰ .·. 3 2̄ 9    **GLASSHOUGHTON**

Tallies Authorising a Person to go underground.

### INSTRUCTIONS

**ON RECEIPT OF THIS ENVELOPE.**

1. Hand the RED disc to the Lampman.

2. Hand the YELLOW disc to the Banksman.

3. Hang the COPPER disc round your neck and retain it all the time you are belowground.

4. Report to the Sub-Control Officer in the Pit Bottom Office immediately you get belowground.

**ON COMPLETION OF DUTY UNDERGROUND.**

1. Report to the Sub-Control Officer in the Pit Bottom Office.

2. On ascending the shaft collect the YELLOW disc from the Banksman.

3. Collect the RED disc from the Lampman.

4. Take the COPPER disc from round your neck and hand all three discs in at the place where you received them.

Identity disc arrangements at Glasshoughton Colliery in NCB times: the instructions are self-explanatory. On the right are some of the discs.

TRANSACTIONS AND RESULTS

OF THE

NATIONAL ASSOCIATION

OF

COAL, LIME, AND IRON-STONE

MINERS

OF GREAT BRITAIN,

HELD AT

LEEDS, NOVEMBER 9, 10, 11, 12, 13, AND 14, 1863.

"Wherever common life and interest is established, then, in the same proportion
as it prevails, there must be the actual surrender of the individual will; what is thus
sacrificed is thrown into the common fund, and unity of being, instead of diversity, is
to the same extent ensured."—GLADSTONE.

LONDON:
LONGMAN, GREEN, LONGMAN, ROBERTS, AND GREEN.
LEEDS:
DAVID GREEN, BOAR LANE.
PRINTED BY F. R. SPARK AND Co., "EXPRESS" OFFICE, LEEDS.

Concern among colliers in regard to their rates of pay was of course of ancient origin and, from the early seventeenth century, the West Riding magistrates had set maximum pay rates. Trades unionism among colliers in West Yorkshire was, as regionally organised, a nineteenth century phenomenon, and a permanent union was only established in 1858. In 1863 the National Association met in West Yorkshire, at Leeds.

Coloured membership certificate of the Yorkshire Miner's (*sic*) Association, formed in 1881 by an amalgamation of the West and South Yorkshire associations. The certificate shows portraits of the leaders of the new Association; the death of the first of these occurred in 1897.

The banner of the Middleton Branch (near Leeds) of the Yorkshire Miners' Association – an organisation formed in 1881.

A Lodge or Branch Union banner from Lofthouse Colliery (opened in 1877 and closed in 1981). The Branch agreed to buy a banner in 1890 and its front face was to be altered in 1896.

Briggs model housing of about 1860: Common Row. The word common alludes to its having been built on common land! In front of the Row is part of the spoil heap of Common Pit.

Briggs' Whitwood village. The colliery wagon shop is on the extreme left, the colliery school to its right, the village institute (now the Rising Sun Inn) in the centre with the village hall in front of it and the long row of colliers' model houses, designed by Voysey, on the right.

## ALLERTON BYWATER COLLIERY.

To E. Shinwell, Esq., M.P.
Secretary for Mines.

Lancaster House,
Doncaster.
*27th June*, 1930.

Sir,

In accordance with the directions of your predecessor in office I have the honour to make the following special Report on the explosion which occurred at Allerton Bywater Colliery, Yorkshire, on 10th March last.

Five men lost their lives in consequence of this explosion: George Paley, Arthur Richards, Albany Taylor, William Townend and John Allan; and another person, Harold Collinson, was slightly injured by the force of the explosion.

Inquest Proceedings.

The Inquests on the bodies of the five men who lost their lives were held by Mr. Will Bentley, H.M. Coroner, Pontefract.

The first day's proceedings were formal identifications, but on the second day nine witnesses were heard and the fullest inquiry made into all matters relevant to the accident.

Messrs. The Airedale Collieries, Ltd., were represented by Mr. H. F. Atter, Solicitor, and the Yorkshire Mine Workers' Association by Mr. A. Smith, Agent, and Mr. H. Smith, President of the Allerton Silkstone Branch.

Mr. George Cook, H.M. Senior Inspector of Mines, and I were present, and throughout the proceedings the Coroner gave me full opportunity to examine all witnesses who were called.

The Jury returned a verdict that death was due in four cases to burns and in the fifth case (John Allan) to injuries, due to an explosion of methane ignited by the firing of a shot, no negligence being attached to anyone.

Descriptive.

The mine is about 1½ miles North of Castleford and is owned by Messrs. Airedale Collieries, Ltd., for whom Mr. H. F. Smithson acts as Agent and Mr. F. W. Milsom as Manager. Employment is given to about 1,400 men belowground and 462 on the surface.

The Silkstone Seam was cut by the shafts at a depth of 312 yards and a rising haulage road approximately three quarters of a mile long led to the Old East District in which the accident occurred.

\# (318)2674 Wt 9163—4327 1375 9/30 E & S A 2

## EXPLOSION AT CRIGGLESTONE COLLIERY, YORKSHIRE

Lancaster House,
Doncaster.
*3rd November, 1941.*

D. R. Grenfell, Esq., C.B.E., J.P., M.P.,
*Secretary for Mines.*

Sir,

In accordance with your instructions, I beg to submit my report on the circumstances of an explosion which occurred at Crigglestone Colliery, Yorkshire, on 29th July, 1941, whereby 22 persons lost their lives and 3 others were injured.

I.—General.

The colliery, owned by Messrs. Benzol & By-Products Ltd., is situated 3½ miles to the South-West of Wakefield. The Agent and Manager is Mr. F. B. Howitt. The seams worked are the Top and Bottom Haigh Moor. The explosion occurred in No. 1 West District, Top Haigh Moor Seam, which is there 256 yards deep. The Bottom Haigh Moor Seam, about 11 yards below, has not been worked anywhere near. The No. 1 West District was opened out by taking forward a narrow bord face from which end faces were developed to right and left. Coal was first produced from these two faces on the 29th April, 1941, and it will be seen from Plan No. 1 that they were 100 and 110 yards long respectively at the time of the explosion. The seam in the district is nearly flat. It is 3 ft. thick with a blue bind roof in which are bands of ironstone and it was undercut in a 4 in. band of dirt. Over the seam is a 4 in. dirt band which generally comes down with the coal.

The district was fully mechanised and electricity was used for coal cutting, drilling, face conveyors, gate conveyors, haulage, a loader, and signalling. Direct current at 500 volts was used for haulage and alternating current at 400 volts for the remainder of the electrical plant.

On the day shift coal was loaded. On the afternoon shift the face conveyors were dismantled, the seam was undercut to a depth of 5 ft. 6 in., shotholes were bored 7 ft. to 9 ft. apart in the coal and as required in the various gate ripping lips, the ripping shots were fired and the packs built. On the night shift shots were fired in the coal, the face conveyors were re-assembled and the gate conveyors moved forward.

There were two deputies in No. 1 West District on the day shift, one deputy and one shot-firer on the afternoon shift, and one deputy and 2 shot-firers on the night shift.

The quantity of air passing into the district as last measured prior to the explosion, on 30th June, 1941, was 10,600 c.f.m., of which 6,450 c.f.m. reached the South Conveyor face. It is well known that the quantity of air circulating in a district, and consequently the percentage of firedamp in the air current, varies considerably during the 24 hours, especially in mechanised districts in thin seams. These fluctuations result from the different kinds of work performed during the cycle and are independent of leakages at doors due to deficiencies or to their being left open. Subsequent to the explosion 7,129 c.f.m. were measured at the entrance to the district, of which only 3,958 c.f.m. reached the South Conveyor face, although in the meantime a brick wall with door inset had been built to prevent direct leakage between intake and return and a door erected in the West main gate.

## REPORT

### On the Causes of, and Circumstances attending the Explosion which occurred at Ingham Colliery, Thornhill, Yorkshire, on the 9th September, 1947

The Right Honourable Hugh Gaitskell, C.B.E., M.P.,
Minister of Fuel and Power. 10 *May*, 1948.

Sir,

I.—INTRODUCTORY

1. In compliance with your direction, I have held a Formal Investigation under the provisions of Section 83 of the Coal Mines Act, 1911, and under the Ministry of Fuel and Power Act, 1945, into the causes of, and circumstances attending, the explosion at Ingham Colliery, Thornhill, Yorkshire, on the 9th September, 1947, causing the loss of 12 lives and injuries to one person. I have now the honour to submit my report.

2. By kind permission of the Mayor and Corporation of Dewsbury, the Inquiry was held in the Council Chamber of the Town Hall, Dewsbury, from the 11th to the 14th November, inclusive, and I desire to record my appreciation of their assistance in placing such suitable accommodation at my disposal.

3. The appearances at the Inquiry were as follows :—

(*a*) *Ministry of Fuel and Power*
Mr. H. J. Humphrys, H.M. Divisional Inspector of Mines.
Mr. E. S. Rees, H.M. District Inspector of Mines.
Mr. G. M. Harvey, H.M. Electrical Inspector of Mines.
Dr. H. F. Coward, Director of Safety in Mines Research and Testing Branch.

(*b*) *National Coal Board*
Mr. J. Hunter, Production Director, North Eastern Division.
Mr. C. H. M. Glover, Legal Adviser, North Eastern Division.
Mr. H. M. Hudspeth, Deputy Production Director, North Eastern Division.

(*c*) *National Union of Mineworkers*
Mr. J. A. Hall, President, Yorkshire Area.
Mr. J. H. Scargill, Secretary, Thornhill Branch.

(*d*) *British Association of Colliery Management*
Mr. A. S. Furniss, Solicitor.

(*e*) *National Association of Colliery Managers*
Mr. A. Holdsworth, President, Yorkshire Branch.

(*f*) *Yorkshire Deputies Association*
Mr. J. Howard.

4. A list of the 25 witnesses examined during the course of the Inquiry is given in Appendix I, and a list of the persons killed and injured in the explosion is given in Appendix II.

(84516)

Some more modern West Yorkshire colliery disasters: the Inspectors of Mines' reports on fatal accidents at:
Allerton Bywater Colliery in 1930, five dead;
Crigglestone Colliery in 1941, twenty-two dead;
Thornhill Colliery in 1947, twelve dead;
Walton Colliery in 1959, five dead;
St John's Colliery in 1959, three dead;
Lofthouse Colliery in 1973, seven dead.
There were of course many other injuries and fatalities.

## Report on the Causes of, and Circumstances attending, the Explosion which occurred at Walton Colliery, Yorkshire, on 22nd April, 1959

*11th September*, 1959.

*The Right Honourable Lord Mills, K.B.E.,*
*Minister of Power.*

My Lord,

1. In accordance with your direction under Section 122 of the Mines and Quarries Act, 1954, I have held a Public Inquiry into the accident which occurred at Walton Colliery, Yorkshire, on 22nd April, 1959, and now have the honour to submit my Report.

2. I find that five men lost their lives in an explosion of firedamp, caused by an electrical arc from a damaged trailing cable and extended by coal dust, in the No. 5 Unit of 10 East District in the Top Haigh Moor Seam.

CONDUCT OF THE INQUIRY

3. I opened the Inquiry at the Town Hall, Wakefield, on 29th June, 1959, and sat until 3rd July, then again from 4th to 12th August. Fifty-two witnesses gave evidence. The following parties were represented:—

*The Ministry of Power* by Mr. H. J. Perrins, O.B.E., H.M. Divisional Inspector of Mines and Quarries ;

*The National Coal Board* by Mr. C. M. H. Glover, Solicitor to the North Eastern Divisional Coal Board ;

*The National Union of Mineworkers* by Mr. J. R. A. Machen, President, Yorkshire Area ;

*The National Association of Colliery Overmen, Deputies and Shotfirers* by Mr. E. Lockett, Secretary, Yorkshire Area ; and

*The National Association of Colliery Managers and the British Association of Colliery Management* by Mr. A. Maurice Smith, Solicitor.

GENERAL PARTICULARS OF WALTON COLLIERY

4. Walton Colliery (formerly known as Sharlston West) is a safety lamp mine situated near Wakefield in the West Riding of Yorkshire ; its general layout, so far as it is relevant to this Report, is shown on Plan No. 1. The colliery employed 1,285 men underground and 298 on the surface, a daily output of 2,200 tons being obtained from the Top Haigh Moor, the Low Haigh Moor, the Kent Thick and the Birkwood or Lidgett Seams. About half of this output was from the Top Haigh Moor.

5. The colliery is owned by the National Coal Board and is situated in the No. 7 (Wakefield) Area of the Board's North Eastern Division. It was managed by G. S. Senior and there were two under-managers, one of whom, H. H. Gregg, had responsibilities which included the working in the Top Haigh Moor seam where the explosion occurred. The Group Manager was T. Dodd and the Area General Manager H. Saul.

1

## REPORT ON THE CAUSES OF, AND CIRCUMSTANCES ATTENDING, THE EXPLOSION WHICH OCCURRED AT ST. JOHN'S COLLIERY, NORMANTON, IN THE WEST RIDING OF YORKSHIRE, ON 26th SEPTEMBER, 1959

*12th December*, 1959

*The Right Honourable Richard Wood, M.P.,*
*Minister of Power.*

Sir,

I—INTRODUCTION

1. In accordance with the direction of your predecessor given under the terms of Section 121 of the Mines and Quarries Act, 1954, I beg to report on the causes of, and circumstances attending, the explosion which occurred in 1's District of the Eleven Yard Seam at St. John's Colliery, Normanton, in the West Riding of Yorkshire, at about 2.0 a.m. on 26th September, 1959.

2. The inquest on the bodies of the three men who died as a result of the accident was opened by Mr. S. H. B. Gill, H.M. Coroner for the Wakefield District in the West Riding of Yorkshire, on 30th September, 1959, and adjourned after the taking of formal evidence of identification. Mr. Gill, sitting with a Jury of seven men, resumed the inquest on 4th November and concluded it on 5th November. The Jury found that death in each case resulted from injuries following an explosion of firedamp which was caused by a spark from a coal drilling machine which was being used to extend a heading in the colliery; and that the same was by misadventure. On 4th and 5th November I attended the inquest, which was searching and exhaustive, and I welcome this opportunity of expressing my appreciation and thanks to H.M. Coroner.

II—GENERAL PARTICULARS OF ST. JOHN'S COLLIERY

3. St. John's Colliery is a safety-lamp mine at Normanton in the West Riding of Yorkshire. At the time of the accident 786 men were employed underground and 209 on the surface; the daily output, obtained from the Silkstone, Eleven Yard, Blocking and Beeston Seams was 1,600 tons, about one-third of which was from the Eleven Yard.

4. The colliery is owned by the National Coal Board and is in the E Group of No. 7 (Wakefield) Area of the Board's North Eastern Division. At the time of the explosion the Group Manager was T. Dodd and the manager of the mine B. H. Hatherton. The workings in the Eleven Yard Seam where the explosion occurred in the right side of 1's Face, were included in the responsibilities of A. S. Harris, one of the two under-managers. At the time of the explosion J. Cotton, overman, appointed by the manager under Section 9 of the Mines and Quarries Act, 1954, was in charge of the mine.

1

## REPORT ON THE CAUSES OF, AND CIRCUMSTANCES ATTENDING, THE INRUSH OF WATER WHICH OCCURRED AT LOFTHOUSE COLLIERY, OUTWOOD, YORKSHIRE, ON 21 MARCH, 1973

Date: 30th August, 1973

The Right Honourable Peter Walker, M.B.E., M.P.,
*Secretary of State for Trade and Industry.*

Sir,

In compliance with your direction, given under Section 122 of the Mines and Quarries Act 1954, I held a Public Inquiry into the accident at Lofthouse Colliery on 21 March, 1973, when seven men were killed. I now have the honour to submit my report.

2. I opened the Inquiry at the No. 1 Crown Court, Wakefield on 30 May, 1973 and it lasted for eight days during which time 61 persons gave evidence. Their names and occupations are given in Appendix I.

3. The interested parties were represented as follows:

*The Department of Trade and Industry*, Mr. R. T. Purvis, H.M. Divisional Inspector of Mines and Quarries, Mr. J. Carver, H.M. Deputy Chief Inspector of Mines and Quarries, Mr. A. Harley, H.M. Senior District Inspector of Mines and Quarries, Mr. S. Luxmore, H.M. Principal Electrical Inspector of Mines and Quarries.

*The National Coal Board*, Dr. H. L. Willett, Deputy Director General (Mining), Mr. T. Wright, Area Director, North Yorkshire Area, Mr. W. Forrest, Chief Mining Engineer, North Yorkshire Area, Mr. T. Mapplebeck, Production Manager, (Manager of the Colliery at the time of the accident).

*The National Union of Mineworkers*, Mr. A. Scargill, Acting General Secretary, Yorkshire Area, Mr. J. T. Leigh, Vice President, Yorkshire Area, Mr. T. McGee, Mining Engineer, Yorkshire Area, Mr. R. Horbury, Financial Secretary, Yorkshire Area, Mr. J. Smart, Area Agent, Yorkshire Area, Mr. A. Hepworth, Chief Administrative Officer, Yorkshire Area, Mr. K. Saunders, Mining Engineer for The National Union of Mineworkers.

*The National Association of Colliery Overmen, Deputies and Shotfirers*, Mr. C. Woods, Agent, Yorkshire Area, Mr. G. Fellows, President, Yorkshire Area, Mr. H. Gregson, Consulting Mining Engineer, Mr. L. Wormald, General Secretary, Yorkshire Area and National President.

*The National Association of Colliery Managers Ltd., and The British Association of Colliery Management*, Sir Andrew Bryan, Consulting Engineer, Mr. C. Alexander, President of The British Association of Colliery Management.

1

Drying the collier's clothes after work, in front of the kitchen fire. Most colliery bathhouses and drying facilities dated from the 1930s and later.

Nostell Long Row: colliers' cottages, probably of the 1860s, belonging to the Winns of Nostell Priory's Nostell Colliery, itself newly enlarged in output.

New Crofton was a colliery housing development by the Lords St Oswald in connection with their new, deep sinkings at Nostell Colliery, opened in 1866. The houses were built from 1880 but did not survive the closure of the colliery in 1987; this photograph of the demolition of a part of them was taken in 1983.

## Low Laithes Colliery.

# SILKSTONE COAL
## PRICE LIST.

|  | s. | d. |
|---|---|---|
| Getting Coal Unriddled "End on," per ton | 1 | 6 |
| Getting Coal Unriddled "Bord," per ton | 1 | 4 |
| Dinting below Bottom Coal 9 feet Gates, 9 inches thick, and stowing in packs, per yard | 1 | 5 |
| Dinting below Bottom Coal 12 feet Gates, 9 inches thick, and stowing in packs per yard | 1 | 10 |
| Dinting below Bottom Coal 9 feet Gates, 9 inches thick, and stowing in packs, per yard, with two fast ends | 2 | 4 |

### STRAIGHT WORK.

|  | s. | d. |
|---|---|---|
| Driving Endings, 9 feet wide, per yard | 2 | 6 |
| Driving Bords, 9 feet to 12 feet wide, per yard | 2 | 0 |
| Breaking in at end on faces, per yard | 2 | 0 |

Bottom Coal to be filled separately.

The same system of deductions for dirt and bad filling as in force at Roundwood Colliery Silkstone Pit.

Thirty per cent is now being paid on the above prices, and is subject to the district advance or reduction, together with any deductions now in force at the above Colliery.

For opening off Banks away from the Main covering off ending, a special allowance will be paid for a period of 12 Months, from this date as under:—

For the first 10 yards 3½d. per ton, without percentage.

For the second 10 yards 2½d. per ton, without percentage.

For the third 10 yards 1½d. per ton, without percentage.

So that after the bank has advanced 30 yards from the covering off Bord, all allowances cease and determine.

Colliers working for a day's wage when called upon ... 4 10

Signed on behalf of the Owners of Low Laithes Colliery,

A. B. BLAKELEY.

Signed on behalf of the workmen of Low Laithes Colliery,

HERBERT HOBSON, Checkweighman.

BETHEL HEMINGWAY, }
ABRAHAM SHEEN, } Committee of the Low Laithes Branch, Miners' Association.
JOSEPH WILKINSON, }

Signed, Saturday, May 30th, 1896.

A price list – an agreement between employers and their men as to the sums to be paid for underground work. This one is for Low Laithes Colliery, Ossett, dated 1896.

# HERONSHAWE MAIN

*The Story of a Yorkshire Colliery*

BY

J. S. FLETCHER

WARD LOCK & CO., LIMITED
LONDON AND MELBOURNE

One of several locally-based colliery novels: *Heronshawe Main*, by J.S. Fletcher (died 1935). It is located in the Castleford area.

A self-explanatory account of a brave action at the Ferry Lane pit in the 1880s.

Moving the axle and spokes of the winding drum at the Ferry Lane pit of the Victoria Coal & Coke Company, near Wakefield, presumably after closure.

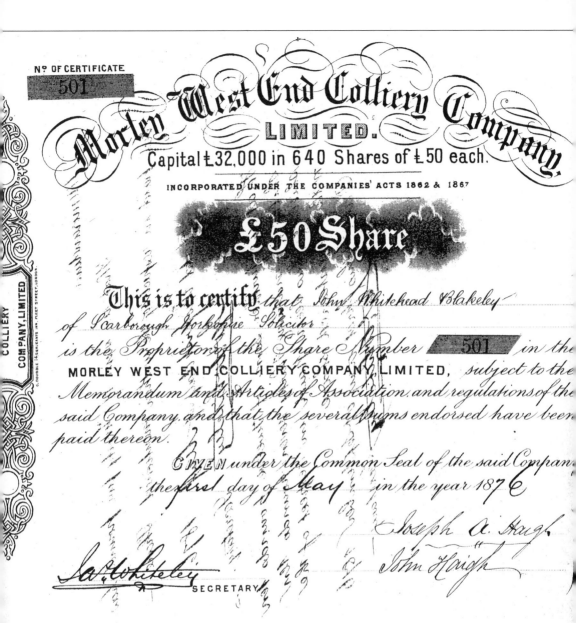

# Morley West End Colliery Company,
## LIMITED.
### Capital £32,000 in 640 Shares of £50 each.

INCORPORATED UNDER THE COMPANIES' ACTS 1862 & 1867

## £50 Share

This is to certify that *John Whitehead Blakeley* of *Scarborough Yorkshire Solicitor* is the Proprietor of the Share Number **501** in the **MORLEY WEST END COLLIERY COMPANY, LIMITED,** subject to the Memorandum and Articles of Association and regulations of the said Company and that the several sums endorsed have been paid thereon.

GIVEN under the Common Seal of the said Company the *first* day of *May* in the year 187*6*

*Joseph A. Haigh*

*John Haigh*

*Jos. Whiteley*
SECRETARY

COLLIERY COMPANY, LIMITED.
C. DOUBLE (4 SERJEANTS INN, FLEET STREET, LONDON.

One of the few colliery company share certificates known to the author as relating to West Yorkshire. The Morley West End Colliery Co. Ltd apparently took over from James Critchley & Sons, established in 1835; in 1903. Confusingly, the concern changed its name to Batley West End. The colliery closed in 1929.

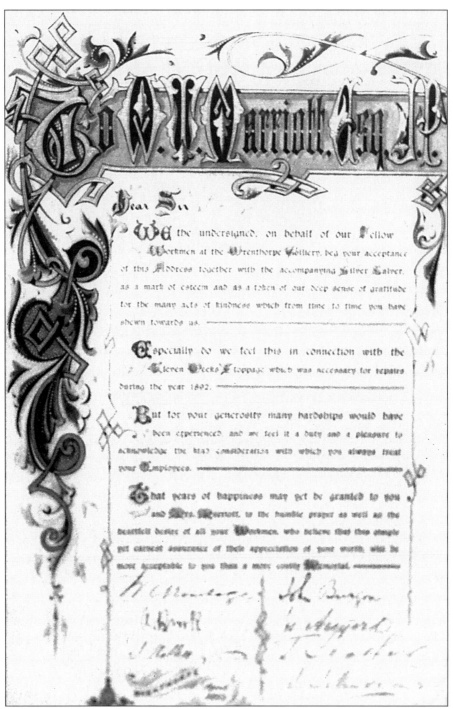

Many coalmasters were by no means ogres to their employees. W.T. Marriott, JP (1822-1899) was a large scale worsted spinner and owner of Wrenthorpe Colliery: here, his colliery workmen present him with an illuminated address on account of gratitude for many kindnesses shown. The colliery closed in 1900, although re-opened later under different owners.

| MEMORANDUMS, OBSERVATIONS, AND APPOINTMENTS, In September, 1863. | SEPTEMBER, NINTH MONTH.—XXX DAYS. [WEEK 37.] |
|---|---|

A colliery owner's diary of 1863, in which he (William Wood, died 1892), owner of St John's (Wakefield) and Fox Holes (Methley) collieries, records visiting his pits, attending a coalmasters' meeting in Leeds and visiting Balaclava Colliery with other coalmasters 'to see the coal cutting machine'. Fox Holes closed in 1901.

A modern commemorative plate for Sharlston Colliery, issued in 1993.

The pony boy and his charge in NCB times.

Colliery fatalities and accidents could be caused as a result of negligence on the part of owners, officials or men – and indeed by nature itself. Here colliers at Victoria Colliery near Morley are warned against the dangerous (but frequent) practice of opening a safety lamp, in 1867.

# CAUTION !

On May 20th, at the Magistrates Room, Dewsbury,

## ANTHONY BOWER,

OF GILDERSOME,

Coal Miner at VICTORIA COLLIERY, Morley,

## WAS COMMITTED TO PRISON FOR FOURTEEN DAYS,

For unlocking and unscrewing the top of his Safety Lamp, on Tuesday, the 14th Inst.

N.B. Any other Person employed at the above Colliery found violating the Colliery Rules will be dealt with accordingly.

BY ORDER.

Victoria Colliery,
Morley, 21st May, 1867.

An early disc coalcutter in West Yorkshire – possibly at Stringers of Clayton West. It was powered by compressed air.

The opening of J.&J. Charlesworths' pithead baths at their Fanny Pit on Rothwell Haigh, near Leeds, in 1934.

Probably the first ever radio broadcast by a brass band from underground was this at Whitwood Colliery pit bottom in November 1924. The Whitwood Colliery Brass Band – augmented – and a comedian, performed, and a temporary stage was built on the lowest of the three decks of the colliery cage.

Henry Briggs (1797-1868) was a Halifax banker's younger son, who, after a short career in textiles, became a coalmaster by marriage to a colliery heiress from Flockton. At Flockton they operated a model social system which included a theatre, sports ground and discussion group, all shared with their colliers' families. Briggs took an interest from 1836 in deeper and hitherto unexploited seams near Castleford, and his Fairies Hill (Whitwood) Colliery opened early in the 1840s, taking advantage of the new railway system. Late in life he saw the introduction of profit-sharing to his collieries – for the first time in Britain on so large a scale, which attracted international interest. He was a Unitarian and a Liberal, and a most able and independent man.

*Left:* A commemorative mug issued at the closure of Denby Grange Colliery.

*Next pages:* An apprenticeship indenture of 1853: a Leeds' widow's son is apprenticed for some four and a half yeras to a lofthouse gate collier.

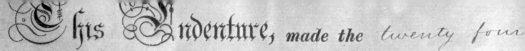

# This Indenture, made the *twenty four*

Year of the Reign of our Sovereign Lady VICTORIA the First, by the Grace of God, of the U~

*H.M.* LORD One Thousand Eight Hundred and *fifty three* BETWEEN *Willia*

*in the County of York, an Infant under the*

*same place Widow the Mother of the said W*

*Thomas Hutchinson of Lofthouse Gate in the parish*

*———————————————————* of the other part; W~

hath of *his* own Free will, and with the Consent of *his said Mother*

to and with the said *Thomas Hutchinson*

*He, &c.* *the date hereof until the first day of August One thousand eight hundred and fifty se~*

~~be fully completed and ended~~; during all which Term the said Apprentice *his* said Mast~

shall do, Fornication or Adultery shall not commit, Hurt or Damage to *his* said Mou~

and forthwith *his* said *Master* thereof warn : Taverns or Alehouses *he* s~

At Dice, Cards, Tables, Bowls or any other unlawful Games *he* shall not play :

without *his* Master's Licence : Matrimony within the said Term shall not contract,

Apprentice shall order and behave *him*-self towards *his* said *Master* and all

*his* said Master's Goods, Chattels, and Money committed to *his* Charge, or which

*his* said Master *his* Executors, Administrators, or Assigns. And the said *Thom*

for *him*-self, *his* Executors, Administrators, and Assigns, doth covenant, promise, and agr~

Apprentice, That *he* the said *Thomas Hutchinson his* —

teach, learn, and instruct *him* the said Apprentice, or cause *him* to be taught, learned,

*——————————————* which the said M*aster* now useth, after the best

find and provide to and for *him* the said Apprentice, sufficient and enough of Meat a~

*to him as such apprentice, during the said*

*the said apprentice the sum of sixpence per week*

*thousand eight hundred and fifty four, the sum*

*from the said first day of August One thousand*

*shillings per week during the residue of the sai*

*best of his ability teach and learn him the said*

And for the true performance of all and singular the Covenants and Agreements aforesaid, each

the Parties above-named to this present Indenture, have set their Hands and Seals the Day and

Day of — _January_ in the _sixteenth_

_dom_ of _Great Britain_ and _Ireland_, QUEEN, Defender of the Faith, and in the Year of our

_John Alcock an infant under the_ of _Leeds_

_twenty one years and Maria Gray of the_

_John Alcock_ —

coal _Miner_ ————————————— of the one part, and

That the said _William John Alcock_ —————

————————— put and bound _him_self Apprentice

———— and with _him_ after the manner of an Apprentice to dwell, remain and serve from

_will attain the age of nineteen years_

for, during, and until the Term of _when the said apprentice_, Years thence next following

_ll_ and faithfully shall serve, _his_ Secrets shall keep, _his_ lawful Commands

shall not do, or consent to be done, but to the utmost of _his_ power shall prevent it,

_nt_ or frequent, unless it be about _his_ Master's — Business there to be done.

of _his_ said _Master_ — shall not waste nor them lend, or give to any person

_his Master's_ Service at any time absent _him_self; but as a true and faithful

_mily_, as well in Words as in Deeds during the said Term : And a true and just Account of all

to _his_ Hands faithfully _he_ shall give at all Times when thereunto required by

_Hutchinson in consideration of the premises_

Presents, to and with the said _Maria Gray and the said_

————————— Executors, Administrators, or Assigns, shall and will

_ted_, in the _Trade or business of a Coal Miner_ ———— And also, shall

_he_ or they may or can, with all circumstances thereunto belonging: And also, shall

_washing lodging and wearing apparel suitable_

_tis of terms and also_ ~~shall~~ _will and shall pay unto_

_the date hereof to the first day of august one_

_ne shilling per week for two years to commence_

_hundred and fifty four and the sum of two_

_prenticeship, and also shall and will_ ~~and~~ _to the_

_rentice to read and write_ —

_and herself_

_ies_ aforesaid doth bind himself unto the other firmly by these Presents. In Witness whereof

_e_-written.

_William John_ _his_ _X_ _Alcock_

_mark_

_Maria Gray_

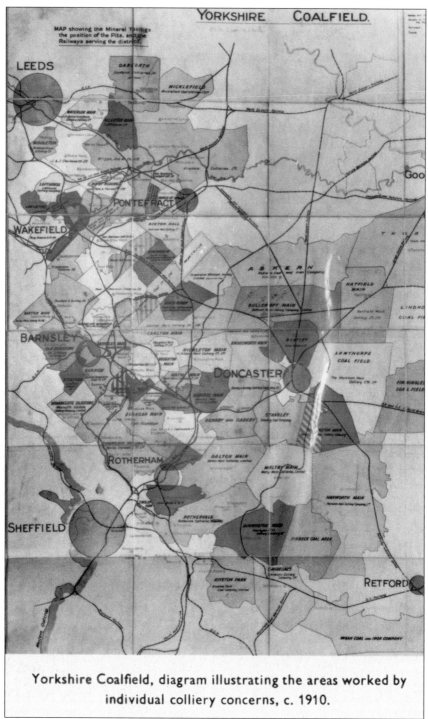

**Yorkshire Coalfield, diagram illustrating the areas worked by individual colliery concerns, c. 1910.**

The Yorkshire coalfield c.1910, showing the areas of coal worked by the larger collieries, and those in the eastern part of the area which were being newly developed. The remaining collieries in the western part of the area were small and obviously considered by the publishers of this diagram as of little consequence.

# Five
# Using the Coal

Extensive scientific trials were carried out at West Riding Colliery, Altofts, which demonstrated conclusively the significance of air-borne dust in colliery explosions. The matter received international attention and it was partly as a result of his experiments that William E. Garforth, the colliery company's managing director, received a knight bachelorhood in 1917.

THE BURNING WELL NEAR PONTEFRACT.

Boring for coal in 1865, in the vicinity of what was developed as George Bradley's Featherstone Manor Colliery. The engraving shows the surface boring structure and the escaping gas, lit by a match.

Sinking gang at one of Denby Grange Colliery's pits – perhaps at Caphouse pit – at the end of the nineteenth century.

Beginning work on the sinking of Ackworth Colliery in 1911; this colliery had no railway connection and was used for manriding.

Although obviously an understanding of where coal and other useful minerals were likely to be found is of ancient origin, the modern scientific study of geology was a popular development of the nineteenth century. This progenitor of the Yorkshire Geological Society was formed in 1837 and the first printed section of the coalfield was produced in 1844 by the Revd Wm Thorp, BA. This was based to a considerable extent on colliery sinkings, and its information was augmented later by yet further sinkings, the work of other geologists and – particularly – the work of the National Geological Survey.

# The Yorkshire College, Leeds.

## DEPARTMENT OF MINING.

The Coal Mining Committee of the Yorkshire College make an urgent appeal to Coal Owners and others in Yorkshire and elsewhere for funds to place the Mining Department of the College on a satisfactory footing. For the past 20 years Classes for underviewers and others employed in coal pits have been held in the College by means of grants for successive periods of three years, made by the Worshipful Company of Drapers of the City of London; but in the opinion of the Committee the time has now come for attempting a more important work, while continuing the old on an extended basis. The College is already in a position to give all the teaching that is needed in Geology, Engineering, Mathematics, Physics, and allied subjects, for satisfactory courses in Coal and Metalliferous Mining: the only desideratum is an adequate department of theoretical and practical Mining. It is thought that the time is opportune for founding a complete School of Mining in connection with the Yorkshire College, and that, as a first step in this direction, it is essential to increase the endowment of the Chair, so as to secure the services of a Professor who will be able to develop the Department in the manner suggested.

The business engagements of Mr. Arnold Lupton, who has conducted the Coal Mining Classes during the past 20 years, having compelled him to withdraw from the Professorship, it is hoped that the opportunity will not be lost of consolidating and extending the department so as to make it rank worthily with the other technical branches of the Yorkshire College, and so become a credit to the county and to the country also.

The Committee have drawn up a scheme of instruction for men actually engaged in Coal Mining operations, who may be unable to spend more than a few hours per week in attendance upon College Classes, and they have also prepared the outlines of a systematic course for students of Mining who are able to give two or three years to the serious study of subjects which will fit them for entering upon all branches of mining work at the end of their academic career. They propose to elaborate this course if they receive from coal owners and others interested in this project a satisfactory amount of encouragement, and they have no reason to doubt that if this be given the Yorkshire College will, in a comparatively short time, have a School of Mining of which its promoters will have reason to be proud.

The Yorkshire College of Science, at Leeds, opened in 1874 and had its own coal mining section. Here an appeal is being made later to form a department with its own professor. The College became Leeds University in 1904.

*Previous page and right:* The Old and New colliery pumping engines at Low Shops, Rothwell Haigh, Leeds. The old engine, on the left, was built by Boulton & Watt for Thomas Fenton, and the first coal rents appear to have been paid in 1787, while the connecting wagonway to the navigable river Aire was probably first used in 1789. The Old Engine was augmented by the colliery's new owners, J.&J. Charlesworth, who took over in 1820, and built the New Engine, of the Cornish type. Both engines worked until 1929, the older one in a brickbuilt house, the later in one of stone.

A wagon type boiler, latterly used for water storage, in the 1960s.

The Union Foundry at Wakefield tenders in 1860 for a 25hp winding engine for Terry Greaves & Co. of Old Roundwood Colliery.

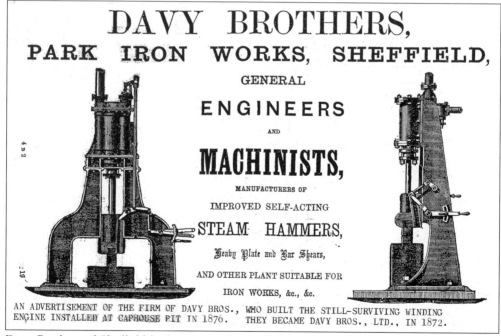

Davy Brothers of Sheffield built many colliery winding engines, including the still-surviving engine at Caphouse Colliery, which now houses the National Coal Mining Museum.

*Above, below and following page:* The lathe at Low Shops workshops of J.&J. Charlesworth at Rothwell Haigh. The lathe was reputedly made by the great engineer Matthew Murray of Leeds, and Charleworths' workshops were capable of work as substantial as the building of locomotives and winding engines.

A locally-built (by Bradley & Craven) winding engine with 41in x 7ft cylinders and a double spiral winding drum, built in 1914 for the Prince of Wales Colliery, Pontefract.

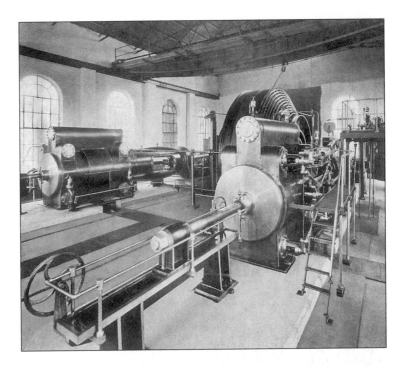

The Bullcliffe Wood Colliery drift with its surface coal conveyor leading up to road access coal screens.

Richard Sutcliffe Ltd's conveyor installation underground at Bullcliffe Wood Colliery, installed there in 1943.

Richard Sutcliffe (1849-1930), a sometime colliery manager, invented and then introduced underground belt coal conveying at Glasshoughton Colliery in 1906.

110

# MESSRS. J & J. CHARLESWORTH L^TD
# ROTHWELL HAIGH COLLIERIES
## STATUTORY RULES & ORDERS 1913
## No. 748.
# SIGNALLING.

92. THE FOLLOWING SIGNALS SHALL BE USED AT ALL TIMES IN CONNECTION WITH WINDING IN SHAFTS: —

(A) FOR WINDING PERSONS: —

1. WHEN A PERSON IS ABOUT TO DESCEND THE BANKSMAN SHALL SIGNAL TO THE ONSETTER - - - 3 BEFORE THE PERSON ENTERS THE CAGE THE ONSETTER SHALL SIGNAL TO THE BANKSMAN AND TO THE WINDING ENGINEMAN - - - - - - WHEN THE PERSON IS IN THE CAGE AND READY TO DESCEND. THE BANKSMAN SHALL SIGNAL TO THE WINDING ENGINEMAN - - - - - - - - - 2

2. WHEN A PERSON IS ABOUT TO ASCEND, THE ONSETTER SHALL SIGNAL TO THE BANKSMAN AND TO THE WINDING ENGINEMAN - - - - - - - 3 BEFORE THE PERSON ENTERS THE CAGE THE

Shaft signalling regulations for the Rothwell Haigh Collieries under legislation of 1913.

*Above and previous page:* The Diamond Coal Cutter Company, using a deep undercut disc cutter, was established in 1897 at Altofts, moved to Normanton in 1898 and to Wakefield in 1902, where it still exists as BJD. About 1900, its published catalogue in French shows that of the seventy-three machines then made, eighteen were for West Yorkshire collieries and eleven were for Pope & Pearson, whose manager W.E. Garforth invented the machine and established the company.

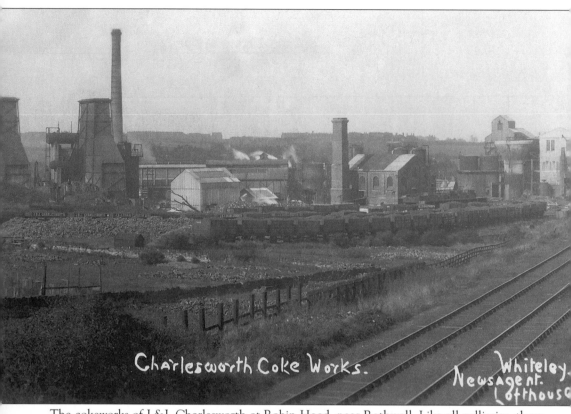

Charlesworth Coke Works.

Whiteley.
Newsagent.
Lofthouse

The cokeworks of J.&J. Charlesworth at Robin Hood, near Rothwell. Like all collieries, those of the Charlesworths were faced with the difficulty of selling large quantities of slack: brickmaking and lime burning were among its uses, but coke-making became of increasing significance in the early nineteenth century. Coke was in fact used for a variety of industrial heating purposes and these modern Simon-Carves coke ovens and by-product ovens were opened in 1900 under an agreement made in 1898; they continued to work into the period of nationalisation.

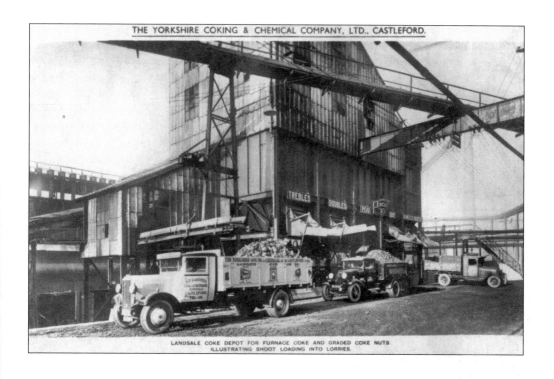

THE YORKSHIRE COKING & CHEMICAL COMPANY, LTD., CASTLEFORD.

LANDSALE COKE DEPOT FOR FURNACE COKE AND GRADED COKE NUTS.
ILLUSTRATING SHOOT LOADING INTO LORRIES.

*Above and below:* The coke and chemical works close to Glasshoughton Colliery consisted of 120 Koppers' kilns, built in 1915 and 1916, and producing coke, tar, sulphate and crude benzol, owned by the Yorkshire Coking & Chemical Co. Ltd.

THE YORKSHIRE COKING & CHEMICAL COMPANY, LTD., CASTLEFORD.

Ferrybridge 'C'

*Above and previous page:* The Ferrybridge 'C' Power Station, near the town and with both rail and water access, used coal brought from local collieries in large compartment boats; it was opened in 1968.

Coal for industry: the only known billhead of the great Leeds Pottery in Hunslet, Leeds.

# Thorp Hall Coals.

## TO BE SOLD

### At the Nether Mills, Steander;

The Waggon Containing Six Tiplers of Coals, Rothwell Haigh Measure.

### Price at the Staith, Ten Shillings and Eight-pence.

*Prices of Carriage, as under, per Waggon.*

|  | s. | d. |
|---|---|---|
| Steander, adjoining new Causeway, and enclosed by the Beck, |  | 0 |
| Water Lane, Stock's Fold, Pork Alley, Weaver's Square, and Muck Lane, |  | 0 |
| Well House Place, and Well Houses, |  | 0 |
| Hill House, and Near Bank, |  | 0 |
| King Street, and Queen Street, |  | 0 |
| Spitalfields, and Cavalier Hill, |  | 0 |
| Far Bank to Mr. Cawood's House, |  | 0 |
| From Mr. Cawood's to Ellerby Lane End, including Black Dog Mill, and Mr. Rhodes' Tan Yard, | } |  |
| New Causeway to Church Gates, and Crown Point, | 1 | 0 |
| Timble Bridge, Garden Street, and Paradise, | 1 | 0 |
| From Timble Bridge, on Marsh Lane, to Sexton Lane End, including Duke Street, to St. Peter's Square, part of York Street, Off Street, and Brick Street, to Sheepscar Beck, on the left, | } 1 | 0 |
| To Ellerby Lane, | 1 | 3 |
| Up Kirkgate to Call Lane End, (if emptied within the Street,) | 1 | 3 |
| From Call Lane End, to Kirkgate End, (if emptied within the Street,) | 1 | 3 |
| High Court Lane, | 1 | 3 |
| On Call Lane, the Calls, Assembly Court, Three Legs Yard, and White Cloth Hall | 1 | 3 |
| To the right of Kirkgate, To Vicar Lane End, including the Vicarage, East Lane, Harper Street, St. James's Church, and part of York Street to Sheepscar Beck, | } 1 | 3 |
| Both Sides Marsh Lane, from Sexton Lane End to Stone's End, | 1 | 3 |
| All within the beginning of St. Peter's Square, to the left of Sheepscar Beck, to Lady Lane Bridge, on Coach Lane, including High Street, and St. Peter's Square. | } 1 | 3 |
| Vicar Lane, Lady Lane to the Bridge, including all to St. Georges' Street, and bounded by Sheepscar Beck, | } 1 | 6 |
| Temple Lane, St. John's Street, Leylands, and Bridge Street, | 1 | 6 |
| From Stone's End on the York Road, to the Riding School, | 1 | 6 |
| On Mabgate adjoining Sheepscar Beck, to Green Row, including Far Fold, Near Fold, and Middle Fold, | } 1 | 8 |
| Bond Street, Commercial Street, Albion Street, to Commercial Street End, Bank Street, Trinity Lane, Boar Lane, Mill Hill, King's Mills, and Swinegate, | } 1 | 8 |
| Albion Street, from Commercial Street End to Upperhead-Row, with Upperhead Row, and Lands Lane to Bond Street, | } 1 | 8 |
| Briggate, Duncan Street, and Lowerhead-Row, | 1 | 8 |
| On Sheepscar Beck, from Lady Lane Bridge, to Stones End, including Quarry Hill, St. Ann's Lane, Stone Flats, Black Flagg's Lane, and Union Row. | } 1 | 8 |

William Fenton the Coal King's new colliery at Waterloo, below Leeds. The sods were cut on the eve of the battle of Waterloo in 1815 and this poster was issued in June 1817. Coal was carried to Leeds in containers on boats, and the inhabitants of Leeds were well served by the new colliery, which supplemented the supply from the Middleton Colliery and several smaller ones. Waterloo Colliery was worked under the Temple Newsam estate.

# LOFTHOUSE,

| | CREDIT s. | d. | | MONEY s. | d. |
|---|---|---|---|---|---|
| Coals ... ... ... ... ... ... | 6 | 0 | ...... | 5 | 9 |
| Riddled Slack... ... ... ... ... | 3 | 9 | ...... | | |

*River Dues on Coals shipped at Bottom Boat, to the Tideway at Goole, 1s. 3d. per Ton; to the Tideway at Selby, 1s. 0¼d. per Ton.*

# ROTHWELL HAIGH,

### LEEDS RIVER.

| | s. | d. | | s. | d. |
|---|---|---|---|---|---|
| Best Coal ... ... ... ... ... | 6 | 0 | ...... | 5 | 9 |
| Seconds Coal ... ... ... ... ... | 4 | 7 | ...... | 4 | 4 |
| Top Coal... ... ... ... ... ... | 5 | 2 | ...... | 5 | 0 |
| Slack Cinders... ... ... ... ... | 7 | 0 | ...... | | |
| Riddled Slack... ... ... ... ... | 3 | 9 | ...... | | |
| Screen Slack ... ... ... ... ... | 2 | 0 | ...... | | |

*River Dues on Rothwell Haigh Coals to the Tideway at Goole, 1s. 4½d. per Ton.*

# SILKSTONE,

### BARNSLEY CANAL.

| | s. | d. | | s. | d. |
|---|---|---|---|---|---|
| Silkstone Coal ... ... ... ... | 6 | 0 | ...... | 5 | 9 |
| Riddled Slack... ... ... ... ... | 3 | 6 | ...... | | |
| Slack Cinders, per Ton ... ... ... | 5 | 0 | ...... | | |

*Canal and River Dues on Silkstone Coal to the Tideway at Goole, 2s. 7½d. per Ton.*

# FLOCKTON,

### AT HORBURY BRIDGE.

| | s. | d. | | s. | d. |
|---|---|---|---|---|---|
| Flockton Coal... ... ... ... ... | 7 | 3 | ...... | 7 | 0 |
| Common Ditto ... ... ... ... | | | ...... | | |
| Riddled Slack... ... ... ... ... | 3 | 6 | ...... | | |

*Canal and River Dues on Flockton Coal to the Tideway at Goole, 2s. 0½d. per Ton.*

# HOLLING HALL,

### WAKEFIELD.

| | s. | d. | | s. | d. |
|---|---|---|---|---|---|
| Winter Coal ... ... ... ... ... | 5 | 6 | ...... | 5 | 3 |
| Bimshaw Coal ... ... ... ... | 4 | 6 | ...... | | |
| Coal Cinders ... ... ... ... ... | 12 | 0 | ...... | | |

*River Dues on Holling Hall Coals to the Tideway at Goole, 1s. 7½d. per Ton.*

# NETHERTON,

THREE MILES ABOVE WAKEFIELD.

|  | CREDIT | | MONEY | |
|---|---|---|---|---|
|  | s. | d. |  | s. | d. |
| Best Coal ... ... ... ... ... | 4 | 9 | ...... | 4 | 6 |
| Lime and Common Coal ... ... | 4 | 0 | ...... | 3 | 9 |
| Engine Coal ... ... ... ... ... | 3 | 0 | ...... | | |

*River Dues on the Netherton Coals to the Tideway at Goole,
1s. 10½d. per Ton.*

# KILNHURST,

RIVER DUNN, NEAR ROTHERHAM.

|  | s. | d. |  | s. | d. |
|---|---|---|---|---|---|
| Nine Feet Coal (for Steam Packets) | 6 | 3 | ...... | 6 | 0 |
| ——Ditto——Hards and Softs...... | 5 | 9 | ...... | 5 | 6 |
| ——Ditto——Softs ... ... ... | 5 | 0 | ...... | 4 | 9 |
| Kent's Main ... ... ... ... ... | 5 | 0 | ...... | 4 | 9 |
| Coal Cinders, *per Dozen*... ... ... | 9 | 6 | ...... | 9 | 0 |
| ——Ditto——*per Ton* ... ... ... | 13 | 0 | ...... | 12 | 6 |
| Riddled Slack... ... ... ... ... | 3 | 0 | ...... | | |
| Unriddled Slack ... ... ... ... | 1 | 6 | ...... | | |

*River Dues on Kilnhurst Coals to the Tideway at Goole, 10d. per Ton.
Do. Do. Slack Do. Do. 5d. „*

Lofthouse, Wakefield, 1848.

*Above and previous page:* The pricelist for the widespread colliery empire of J.&J. Charlesworth, established by 1773 and existing until 1947: it is dated 1848 and shows the geographical range of the collieries then worked by the firm in the West and South Yorkshire coalfields.

MORLEY MAIN COLLIERY,

*SEPT. 27th, 1871.*

On Account of the Reductions made in the Selling Prices of our Coal since 1867, we shall make a General Advance as follows:

Best, Seconds, Softs, Thirds, Engine Coal, Nutts; also, Best Little Coal, Gas Coal, Furnace Coal and Undressed Little Coal, 1s. per Ton advance on your present Prices; and 6d. per Ton on Engine Slack will take place on and after October 2nd, 1871.

Thanking you for past favours, and hoping to have a continuance of the same.

We remain,

Yours truly,

Wm. ACKROYD & BROS.

Morley Main Colliery coal types and prices were to be increased in a boom period, 1871.

The offices of the Victoria Coal & Coke Co. Ltd in Southgate, Wakefield. In the garden was a huge piece of coal extracted for display in a great exhibition. The author well recollects accompanying his parents to pay their coal accounts here.

A new boiler made in 1901 by a Wakefield firm of boilermakers for Whitwood Collieries.

## PRICES of CAST IRON GOODS,
### *At the Low-Moor Iron-Works, near* Bradford, *Yorkshire.*
September 1st, 1799.

| | Per Cwt. | | | Per Cwt. | |
|---|---|---|---|---|---|
| | s. | d. | | s. | d. |
| Cylinders and working Barrels, bored | | | Ditto, Octagon - - - - - | 42 | 0 |
| 18 Inches and upwards - - - | 28 | 0 | Ditto, flued - - - - - | 44 | 0 |
| Ditto, under 18 Inches - - | 30 | 0 | Cast Iron Boilers - - - - | 18 | 0 |
| Cylinder Cups and Bottoms - - | 22 | 0 | Steam and injection Boxes - - | 25 | 0 |
| Ditto, turned - - - - | 28 | 0 | Common Mill Work, from 14s. to | 16 | 0 |
| Pipes, elbowed and branched - | 18 | 0 | Common Spur Wheels 56lb & upwards | 14 | 0 |
| Bucket and clack pierced windbores | 18 | 0 | Ditto under 56lb. - - - - | 15 | 0 |
| Plain Pipes above 8 Inches - | 15 | 0 | Bevil'd ditto, 56lb. and upwards | 16 | 4 |
| Ditto 8 Inches to 4 Inches - | 16 | 4 | Do. under 56lb. & Sun and Planet Wheels | 18 | 8 |
| Ditto under 4 Inches - - | 21 | 0 | Pedestals, Cps, Hummer Blocks, &c. | 16 | 4 |
| Pistons and Pistons Rings unturned | 18 | 0 | Circular Couplings and Catch Boxe | 16 | 4 |
| Ditto, turned, from 25s. to - - | 28 | 0 | Shafts unturned, Pillars & Head stocks | 14 | 0 |
| Receivers, Regulators, & Sinking Pipes | 21 | 0 | Tappet Wheels - - - - - | 14 | 0 |
| Balance Wheels - - - - | 13 | 0 | Corfe and Tram Wheels - - - | 18 | 8 |
| Joints, Bosses, Gudgeons and Steps | 14 | 0 | Flanged Waggon Wheels - - - | 14 | 0 |
| Crank and Octagon Wheels - - | 14 | 0 | Other kind of waggon wheels, from 16s. to | 21 | 0 |
| Grate Bars - - - - - | 12 | 0 | Rails for waggon roads, 20lb. per lingle | | |
| Frames and Doors fitted - - | 16 | 4 | yard, and under - - - - | 14 | 0 |
| Buckets - - - - - | 18 | 8 | Above 20lb. and under 30lb. | 13 | 0 |
| Wrought Iron Boilers, round, plain, | | | 30lb. and upwards - - - | 12 | 0 |
| from 40s. to - - - - | 42 | 0 | | | |

An early pricelist of work produced at the Low Moor Iron Works, dated 1799: already, only eight years after opening, it was offering steam engine parts and colliery equipment.

The introduction of the use of coke in the iron smelting blast furnace developed from the 1780s in the West Riding. The numerous earlier iron furnaces had used charcoal. The use of locally-occurring ironstone (particularly but not exclusively the Black Bed ironstone around Bradford, which produced some 1,000 tons per acre and contained up to 33% iron) with a coke blast, occurred from 1783 at Birkenshaw, and some of the blast furnaces of West Yorkshire were to work long into the twentieth century. The availability of suitable limestone for flux purposes was of additional benefit. Shelf Ironworks, shown here, were on land bought in 1794, and ceased production in 1849.

## Leeds Crown-Glass.

*Fixtures of Prices commencing January 1, 1787.*

|  | l. | s. | d. |
|---|---|---|---|
| Best, *per Case*, of 24 Tables, | 8 | 8 | 0 |
| Seconds, Ditto, | 7 | 4 | 0 |
| Thirds, Ditto, | 6 | 12 | 0 |
| Quarries, 12 s. and 14 s. *per Foot*, |  |  | 4 |
| Ditto, - - - - 9 s. |  |  | 4½ |

SQUARES, containing 35 Inches, and under, *per Foot*, 5
- - - - - From 35 to 48 inclusive, Do. 6
- - - - - 48 to 72 Ditto - 7
- - - - - 72 to 108 Ditto, - 8
- - - - - 108 to 120 Ditto, - 10
- - - - - 120 to 144 Ditto, - 12
- - - - - 144 to 180 Ditto, - 14
- - - - - 180 to 216 Ditto, - 16
- - - - - 216 to 288 Ditto, - 18
And to advance according to Size in Proportion.

RANGES, not more than 6 Inches broad, *per Foot*, 5¼
Ditto, - - - 7½ Ditto, - 6½
Ditto, - - - 8 Ditto, - 7½
Ditto, - - - 8½ Ditto, - 8
Ditto, - - - 9 Ditto, - 8½
All above as many Pence per Foot as Inches in Breadth.

Table-Crates, unboarded, 18d. each, if boarded, 2s.
Range-Crates, to contain 200 Foot, 2s. 6d. each.
Boxes, containing 200 or 240 Foot Squares, 2s. 6d. each; and Sash Boxes according to Size.

Local coal was used within the industrialised, coal-bearing parts of the coalfield for a wide range of purposes; domestic, steam-raising, textile processing, limeburning, iron making and working, brick, clay and glassmaking, among others. This is a list of the prices of window glass (glass bottle prices are on the other side) at Leeds in 1787.

*Above and below:* Many industries in West Yorkshire relied on local collieries for their basic power-producing material, coal. Glass was produced in the area from the sixteenth century at least, and in the case of Glasshoughton, near Castleford, a glassworks established about 1690 gave the forepart of the village's name. Here the glassworks were able to combine the use of immediately-available coal, sand and lime in their product, although later imported sand, which produced white instead of green glass, was much used. Edgar Breffit's huge glassworks at Castleford was one of the largest in the world for making glass containers; the works were established in 1836.

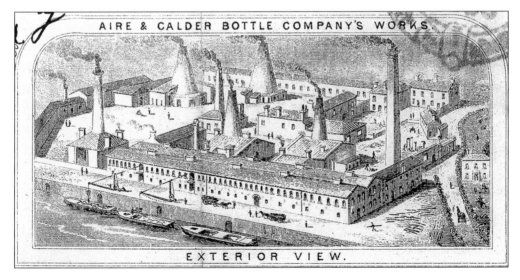

## Dirtcar Colliery, near Wakefield.

*May 16/62* 1 6 5

M: *John Beaumont*

## Bought of Moore and Milthorp.

| | Tons. | Cwts. | Rate. | £ | s. | D. |
|---|---|---|---|---|---|---|
| WINTER COAL ............ | 2 | 1 | | | 8 | 6 |
| SECONDS ... ............. | | | | | | |
| ENGINE....................... | | | | | | |
| SLACK....................... | | | | | | |
| SMUDGE ................. | | | | | 8 | 6 |

*Rec'd 17/- 16 May 1862*

*W Beaumount*

£ *17 - 0*

*Above and below:* Nineteenth-century customers' coal bills from small West Yorkshire collieries, sold in (road) wagon loads and by tonnage, respectively.

## New Park, near Wakefield.

*Mar 10* 18 *34*

Delivered to *Wm Ellwall* ½ Waggons

of *Coal End* from the Colliery of John Woollin,

on Account of *W Marsden* £ s. d.

at *16/-* per Waggon ...............

*12/-*

£ *14 - 0*

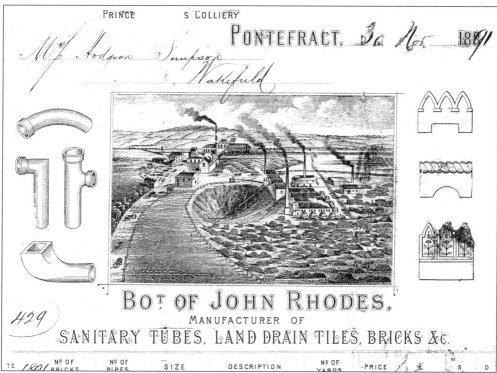

Locally-occurring clays had been used in medieval times for the manufacture of pots, and from the seventeenth century also for the making of bricks and roofing tiles. The regional pottery-making industry grew in the later eighteenth century to serve international markets, although for its fine wares it increasingly used fine clays from the South West, with local coal. Industrialisation and the growth of house building led to a vast expansion of brickmaking too, and numbers of collieries had their own brickworks, such as this one operated by John Rhodes at the Prince of Wales Colliery adjoining Pontefract: coal slack produced at the colliery fired the kilns.

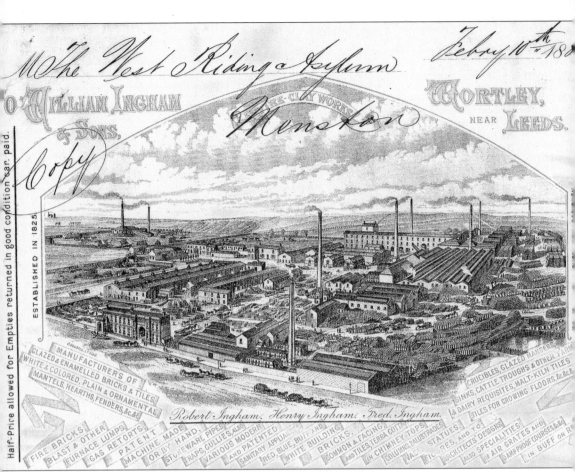

The Wortley fireclay works, established in 1825, survived to be amalgamated into the new Leeds Fireclay Company in 1889. They had their own coal and clay mines: one of their horsedrawn supply railways is shown on this engraved billhead used in 1886.